Basics of
Qualitative
Research

We dedicate this book to Barney Glaser
with admiration and appreciation.

Anselm Strauss
Juliet Corbin

Basics of Qualitative Research

Grounded
Theory
Procedures and
Techniques

SAGE Publications
International Educational and Professional Publisher
Newbury Park   London   New Delhi

For information address:

SAGE Publications, Inc.
2455 Teller Road
Newbury Park, California 91320
E-mail: order@sagepub.com

SAGE Publications Ltd.
6 Bonhill Street
London EC2A 4PU
United Kingdom

SAGE Publications India Pvt. Ltd.
M-32 Market
Greater Kailash I
New Delhi 110 048 India

Printed in the United States of America

Library of Congress Cataloging-in-Publication Data

Strauss, Anselm L.
    Basics of qualitative research: grounded theory procedures and
techniques / Anselm Strauss and Juliet Corbin.
        p. cm.
    Includes bibliographical references and index.
    ISBN 0-8039-3250-2.—ISBN 0-8039-3251-0
    1. Social sciences—Statistical methods. I. Corbin, Juliet M.,
1942- . II. Title.
    HA29.S823 1990
    300'.72—dc20   90-39609
                                                    CIP

96 97 98 99 20 19

Sage Production Editor: Susan McElroy

Contents

104/12

If the artist does not perfect a new vision in his process of doing, he acts mechanically and repeats some old model fixed like a blue print in his mind.

John Dewey, *Art as Experience*, 1935, p. 50

Preface

This book is addressed to researchers in various disciplines
(social science and professional) who are interested in inductively building theory, through the qualitative analysis of data.
However exciting may be their experiences while gathering
data, there comes a time when the data must be analyzed. Often
researchers are perplexed by this necessary task. They are dis-
mayed not only by the sheer number of fieldnote, document, or
interview pages ("mountains of data") now confronting them,
but are often troubled by the following questions. How can I
make sense out of all of this material? How can I have a theoretical interpretation while still grounding it in the empirical
reality reflected by my materials? How can I make sure that my
data and interpretations are valid and reliable? How do I break
through the inevitable biases, prejudices, and stereotypical perspectives that I bring with me to the analytic situation? How do
I pull all of my analysis together to create a concise theoretical
formulation of the area under study?

7

The purpose of this book is to answer these and other questions related to qualitative interpretation of data. It is written in a clear and straightforward manner. It is intended primarily to provide the basic knowledge and procedures needed by persons who are about to embark upon their first qualitative analysis research project and who want to build theory at the substantive level.

The mode of qualitative analysis guiding our discussion is known as the "grounded theory" approach, or "method" as it is sometimes called. This is the fourth in a series of books on grounded theory. The first, *The Discovery of Grounded Theory* (Glaser & Strauss, 1967), presented both the argument and underlying logic for the procedures discussed in this and the other books. As such, it is still useful and prerequisite reading to any of the texts. The second book, *Theoretical Sensitivity* (Glaser, 1978), and the third, *Qualitative Analysis for Social Scientists* (Strauss, 1987), were designed to be read and used by somewhat more advanced researchers than this book. Though the latter was especially written for beginners, we anticipate that even the more experienced researchers will find additional answers to some of their longstanding and unanswered questions.

If you read and study *each* of these books, which we strongly advocate, you will find that some of their terminology and specific recommended procedures are not always identical. Mainly, this is because of the additional reflection but also because of different experiences resting both on teaching and our specific research projects. When comparing Glaser's *Theoretical Sensitivity* and Strauss' *Qualitative Analysis for Social Scientists* and this book, you will find some further terminological and procedural differences. Basically, however, all of the books express an identical stance toward qualitative analysis and suggest the same basic procedures. This book does spell out the procedures and techniques (the subtitle of this book) in greatest detail and in the step-by-step fashion that we now believe is most useful for *learning* qualitative analysis.

All of these books are based on the vivid experiences of those who have done and taught qualitative research and analysis in seminars and consultations for many years. The books collectively offer one approach to doing qualitative analysis and their purpose is very specific: that of building theory. The philosophic beliefs and the scientific tradition that underlie the books give rise to their mission of building theory through qualitative research. Formulating theoretical interpretations of data grounded in reality provides a powerful means both for understanding the world "out there" and for developing action strategies that will allow for some measure of control over it.

In addition to reading and studying the method books, we believe that your understanding of grounded theory would be greatly enhanced through study of some of the monographs written by Glaser, Strauss, and associates. These include *Awareness of Dying* (Glaser & Strauss, 1965); *Time for Dying* (Glaser & Strauss, 1968); *Experts Versus Laymen: A Study of the Patsy and the Sub-Contractor* (Glaser, 1976); *The Social Organization of Medical Work* (Strauss, Fagerhaugh, Suczek, & Wiener, 1985); and *Unending Work and Care* (Corbin & Strauss, 1988b).

The analytic mode at the heart of this book is learnable by anyone who will take the trouble to study its procedures. Like any set of practices, the level of accomplishment will vary among users. On the other hand, the practices learned in this book may prove useful in ways originally unanticipated by either writers or readers. As remarked earlier by Strauss (1987, p. xiii) when referring to the analytic process, "Like any set of skills, the learning involves hard work, persistence, and some, not always entirely, pleasurable experiences." To be sure, it is often immensely exciting and enjoyable too. Furthermore, these experiences are requisite to discovering how to use and adapt any method—including grounded theory. The use and adaptation will inevitably be a "composite of situational contexts, and for [developing] a personal [research] biography, astuteness [in doing the work], plus theoretical and social sensitivity. On top of this, to complete any research project, one needs a bit of luck and courage" (Strauss, 1987, p. xiii).

Overview of the Contents

This book is broken down into three major parts. Part I provides an overview of the operational logic behind the use of grounded theory. It includes Chapters 1 through 4. Part II details the specific analytic techniques and procedures of the method. This section is made up of Chapters 5 through 11. The final section, Part III, explains the important adjunct procedures that accompany the collection and analysis of data. Included here are Chapters 12 through 14.

To take each chapter now separately, Chapter 1 employs a question and answer format to acquaint the reader with the differences between grounded theory research and modes of analysis from other types of qualitative research. It explains its origins and philosophical foundations, as well as responds to some of the inquiries most often made by students about to embark on their first grounded theory study.

Chapter 2 is titled "Getting Started" and its purpose is just that, to provide the student with the basic components needed to begin a grounded theory study. In this chapter, we present suggestions on how to identify sources of researchable problems and offer guidelines for framing the research question.

In Chapter 3, we explain what we mean by the term *theoretical sensitivity*, a very important concept in grounded theory methodology. We also explore how one might maintain a balance between being creative, a necessary component of theory development, and doing "good science," which after all is the purpose behind doing any research study.

Chapter 4 discusses the uses of literature in grounded theory studies and dispels some of the myths that have developed over the years about its usage. It does so by explaining how one might use one's reading and experience to gain theoretical sensitivity and to develop concepts that are, later, validated against actual data.

Chapter 5, the first chapter on analysis, describes the process of open coding. We take the reader step-by-step through the procedures beginning with concept labeling; moving on to how concepts are grouped to form categories; then on to how to name categories; finally, we end our discussion with a section on how to develop categories in terms of their properties and the dimensional ranges over which properties might vary.

Chapter 6, is, we believe, one of the most important chapters. In it we offer techniques that allow users to break through biases and standard ways of thinking about data; thus enabling them to think about data in new ways. This is a must for anyone wanting to think creatively about phenomena, while still wishing to ground findings in reality.

In Chapter 7, we move on to axial coding—our second type of coding. Here we describe how categories are related to their subcategories by means of a model we call the "paradigm." Also included in this chapter is an important short section describing how an analyst makes use of both inductive and deductive thinking to arrive at and check out hypotheses regarding possible relationships between a category and its subcategories.

Selective coding, the coding procedure described in Chapter 8, explains how major categories are integrated; and how variation is achieved in the theory by grouping categories according to their specific dimensional locations. Chapter 9 on process, shows how change and movement can be brought into the theory.

Chapter 10 presents a framework for how one might tightly integrate conditions and consequences into the theory by linking them to a phenomenon through action/interaction. The chapter is meant for the more advanced analysts, but there is also much in it of value for beginners. A brief section is included at the end in which we discuss the differences between formal and substantive theory.

Chapter 11, "Theoretical Sampling," explains how one samples in grounded theory method. Specifically, it shows how sampling differs according to the type of coding—open, axial, or selective—that one is engaged in.

The role of memos and diagrams is explored in Chapter 12. These helpful devices are used to keep track of the products of one's analysis, and grow in depth and degree of abstractness as one moves through the coding process. In Chapter 13, we take up the very important issues of presenting and writing about grounded theory studies in books, journals, and dissertations.

The final chapter, Chapter 14, presents criteria for evaluating grounded theory studies. This chapter should be extremely useful, not only for persons wishing to critique their own and others' work, but also those who review articles for journal publications and for funding agencies.

A Concluding Note

After writing a draft of this book and using it to teach graduate students and advanced researchers, it was pointed out to us that the book had value beyond the use for which it was designed—teaching students how to do grounded theory studies.

It also has potential use for those wishing to do theme analysis either alone or in conjunction with quantitative studies. Those interested in concept development might find the information we give in certain chapters helpful. Persons just interested in new ways of thinking about phenomena might also find parts of the book worthwhile. These different groups of readers need not study or practice all that we've described in this book, but limit their reading to Chapters 1 through 6 or 7. They may also want to peruse Chapters 11 and 12.

Persons serving on review boards of journals or funding agencies often encounter reports on grounded theory studies or proposals. They might want to skim the entire book to gain some understanding of the terminology that is used and the basic procedures of the method; then focus on Chapter 14, where we describe the criteria that can be used to evaluate written grounded theory research reports or proposals.

Scholars interested in theory development, both inductive and deductive, might find certain parts of the book useful for supplementing their own methods. We ourselves are open to all these possible uses. We only hope that those who use this book learn as much from reading it as we did writing it.

A last note: you will find that all through the book a special system of italicizing and using bold print has been used. *Italics* are used to call attention to the special concepts and terminology of grounded theory method—like "categories," "dimensions," and "theoretical sensitivity." We have tried not to over use italics but have used them freely. **Bold print** is used for certain terms and phrases, as well as for entire sentences. The bolded sentences should be useful on repeated scanning or reading of the text, since they are quickly visible. Bolded terms and phrases are used for the same reason. They are also used to bring out special terms used in case illustrations. It is in the illustrative pages that perhaps you will find some inconsistency in our system; but please bear with us, since generally it should work well for you.

We wish to express our gratitude to several students and colleagues who reviewed and critiqued the drafts of this book. We especially thank Jill Rhine, Anna Hazan, and Lora Lempert for their thoughtful and specific comments on a later draft. We also thank Denise Burnette, Theresa Montini, Cheryl Hall, and Kathy Slobin, for their reviews of an early draft, as well as Joan Fujimura at Harvard University and Leigh Star at the University of California, Irvine for using the book with their students. All of their comments were invaluable in making the revisions necessary to improve the clarity, quality, and usefulness of the book. Also important were the criticisms made by Setsuo Mizuno of the University of Hosei, Tokyo, Japan, and Dick Corbin, an engineer in Silicon Valley. We also want to thank Salmonica Maeth for the many hours that she spent typing and retyping the manuscript. Most of all, we express our grateful appreciation to Barney Glaser, who, with Anselm Strauss, began it all with their intense nightly phone conversations about their evolving research methods that now go by the name of "grounded theory."

Part I

Basic Considerations

Discovery has been the aim of science since the dawn of the Renaissance. But how those discoveries are made have varied with the nature of the materials being studied and the times. Galileo, in the following quotation describes his method for making discoveries:

> The method is this: direct the telescope upon the sun as if you were going to observe that body. Having focused and steadied it, expose a flat white sheet of paper about a foot from the concave lens; upon this will fall a circular image of the sun's disk, with all the spots that are on it arranged and disposed with exactly the same symmetry as in the sun. The more the paper is moved away from the tube, the larger this image will become, and the better the spots will be depicted. (Drake, 1957, p. 115)

Although we are studying more worldly, though often just as elusive objects as the sun and stars (persons, groups, and collectives, acting and interacting alone and together) we, like Galileo, have an effective method for discovery. But, before discussing the actual analytic procedures that comprise it, we ask you to examine closely the chapters in Part I. These next four chapters are our way of giving you a "telescope" to see with. They provide you with the basic operative logic that lies behind the grounded theory method, so that you might more clearly understand what you are doing and why you are doing it.

Introduction

Before moving into the more technical aspects of doing analysis (as presented in this book from Chapter 5 on) it is helpful to have some background information about qualitative analysis in general and grounded theory in particular. In this chapter, the information will be presented in the form of questions and answers, the questions being derived from those most often asked by beginning researchers.

What Is Qualitative Research?

By the term *qualitative research* we mean any kind of research that produces findings not arrived at by means of statistical procedures or other means of quantification. It can refer to research about persons' lives, stories, behavior, but also about organizational functioning, social movements, or interactional relationships. Some of the data may be quantified as with census data but the analysis itself is a qualitative one. Actually, the term *qualitative research* is confusing because it can mean different things to different people. Some researchers gather data by means of interview and observation—techniques normally associated with qualitative methods. However, they then code that data in a manner that allows them to be statistically analyzed. They are in effect quantifying qualitative data. *Notice,* however, we are not referring to this process, but to a **non**mathematical analytic procedure that results in findings derived from data gathered by a variety of means. These include observations and interviews, but might also include documents, books, videotapes, and even data that have been quantified for other purposes such as census data.

What Kind of Skills Are Required for Doing Qualitative Research?

The requisite skills for doing qualitative research (as you will later see) are these: to step back and critically analyze situations, to recognize and avoid bias, to obtain valid and reliable data, and to think abstractly. To do these, a qualitative researcher requires theoretical and social sensitivity, the ability to maintain analytical distance while at the same time drawing upon past experience and theoretical knowledge to interpret what is seen, astute powers of observation, and good interactional skills.

Can I Combine Qualitative and Quantitative Methods?

The answer is yes. The two types of methods can be used effectively in the same research project (Strauss, Bucher, Enrlich, Schatzman, & Sabshin, 1964). Most research projects and researchers, however, place their emphasis on one form or another, partly out of conviction, but also because of training and the nature of the problems studied. Examples of how the two can be combined are as follows. One might use qualitative data to illustrate or clarify quantitatively derived findings; or, one could quantify demographic findings. Or, use some form of quantitative data to partially validate one's qualitative analysis (see Denzin, 1970, on "triangulation").

Why Do Qualitative Research?

There are many valid reasons for doing qualitative research. One reason is the conviction of the researcher based upon research experience. Some researchers also come from a scientific discipline, such as anthropology, or adhere to a philosophical orientation, such as phenomenology, both of which traditionally advocate the use of qualitative methods for data gathering and analysis, whose use has given satisfactory results. Another reason is the nature of the research problem. Some areas of study naturally lend themselves more to qualitative types of research, for instance, research that attempts to uncover the nature of persons' experiences with a phenomenon, like illness, religious conversion, or addiction. Qualitative methods can be used to uncover and understand what lies behind any phenomenon about which little is yet known. It can be used to gain novel and fresh slants on things about which quite a bit is already known. Also, qualitative methods can give the intricate details of phenomena that are difficult to convey with quantitative methods.

Who Does Qualitative Research?

Qualitative research is done by researchers in the social and behavioral sciences, as well as by practitioners in fields that concern themselves with issues related to human behavior and functioning. This style of research can be used to study organizations, groups, and individuals. It can be carried out by research teams or by persons acting in pairs, or alone. When qualitative methods are combined with quantitative ones, the qualitative aspect is usually subsidiary to the larger research project and is likely to be carried out by individuals or a small team of specialists.

What Are the Major Components of Qualitative Research?

Basically, there are three major components. First there are the **data**, which as mentioned can come from various sources. Interviews and observations are the most common sources.

The second component of qualitative research consists of the different **analytic** or **interpretive procedures** that are used to arrive at findings or theories. These procedures include the techniques for conceptualizing data. This process, called "coding," varies by the training, experience, and purpose of the researcher. See, for example, Becker (1970), Charmaz (1983), Lofland (1971), and Miles and Huberman (1984). Other procedures are also part of the analytic process. These include nonstatistical sampling (see Schatzman & Strauss, 1973), the writing of memos, and diagramming of conceptual relationships.

Written and **verbal reports** make up the third component of qualitative research. These may be presented in scientific journals or conferences and take various forms depending upon the audience and the aspect of the findings or theory being presented. For instance, someone may present either an overview of the entire findings or an in-depth discussion of one part of the study.

Are There Different Types of Qualitative Research?

This question has different answers depending upon what is really being asked. For example, is it types of research that one is asking about, or purposes, or approaches guiding analysis?

Often when describing qualitative research, types, purposes, and approaches to analysis become confused and mixed up in the description.

Some of the different types of qualitative research are: grounded theory, ethnography, the phenomenological approach, life histories, and conversational analysis. These types can be and are used by researchers of different disciplines. For instance, nurses, anthropologists, or sociologists may use ethnography to study a problem related to their discipline, just as they could use grounded theory or life histories.

When it comes to purposes, these don't appreciably differ for different researchers. The research findings may be used to: clarify and illustrate quantitative findings, build research instruments, develop policy, evaluate programs, provide information for commercial purposes, guide practitioners' practices, and serve political ends, as well as for more scientific purposes such as the development of basic knowledge.

Also, one of the major controversies and questions concerning qualitative research pertains to the question of approach. Or, how much interpretation should there be of data? Some researchers believe that data **should not be analyzed**, per se; but rather the researcher's task is to gather the data and present them in such a manner that "the informants speak for themselves." The aim is to give an honest account with little or no interpretation of—interference with—those spoken words or of the observations made by the researcher. While this particular group of researchers hold that the informants' views of reality may not reflect the "truth," nevertheless the subjects' views are reported in the spontaneous and meaningful ways that they were actually expressed. The philosophical principle underlying this approach is that by presenting this faithful account, the researcher's biases and presence will not intrude upon the data. In this perspective, the researcher's scholarly obligation is to hear and report, somewhat akin to a journalist.

Other qualitative researchers are concerned with **accurate description**, when doing their analysis and presenting their findings. Because the investigator cannot possibly present all the data en toto to the readers, it is necessary to reduce these data. The principle here is to present an accurate description of what is being studied, though not necessarily all of the data that have been studied. Reducing and ordering materials of course represents selection and interpretation. The researchers who advocate or primarily produce accurate description also typically intersperse their own interpretive comments in and around long descriptive passages and the quotations from interview fieldnotes. Many researchers develop great skill in weaving descriptions, speakers' words, fieldnote quotations, and their own interpretations into a rich and believable descriptive narrative. The illustrative materials are meant to give a sense of what the observed world is really like; while the researcher's interpretations are meant to represent a more detached conceptualization of that reality. The interpretations made of the descriptive material vary in their level of abstraction, as presented by different researchers and perhaps also within the same publication. Not all the interpretive commentary is, strictly speaking, theoretical in nature but some researchers have this as part of their aim.

Still other investigators are concerned with **building theory**. They believe that the development of theoretically informed interpretations is the most powerful way to bring reality to light (Blumer, 1969; Diesing, 1971; Glaser, 1978). Building theory, by its very nature, implies interpreting data, for the data must be conceptualized and the concepts related to form a theoretical rendition of reality (a reality that cannot actually be known, but is always interpreted). The theoretical formulation that results not only can be used to explain that reality but provides a framework for action. Researchers concerned with building theory also believe that theories represent the most systematic way of building, synthesizing, and integrating scientific knowledge.

What Is a Grounded Theory?

A **grounded theory** is one that is inductively derived from the study of the phenomenon it represents. That is, it is discovered, developed, and provisionally verified through systematic data collection and analysis of data pertaining to that phenomenon. Therefore, data collection, analysis, and theory stand in reciprocal relationship with each other. One does not begin with a theory, then prove it. Rather, one begins with an area of study and what is relevant to that area is allowed to emerge.

Why Build Theory That Is Grounded?

A well-constructed grounded theory will meet four central criteria for judging the applicability of theory to a phenomenon: **fit, understanding, generality**, and **control**. (See Glaser & Strauss, 1967, pp. 237-250, and also Glaser, 1978, p. 3, for a more thorough discussion of this, and also for the characteristics of theory that either is not at all or is adequately grounded.) If theory is faithful to the everyday reality of the substantive area and carefully induced from diverse data, then it should fit that substantive area. Because it represents that reality, it should also be comprehensible and make sense both to the persons who were studied and to those practicing in that area. If the data upon which it is based are comprehensive and the interpretations conceptual and broad, then the theory should be abstract enough and include sufficient variation to make it applicable to a variety of contexts related to that phenomenon. Finally, the theory should provide control with regard to action toward the phenomenon. This is because the hypotheses proposing relationships among concepts—which later may be used to guide action—are systematically derived from actual data related to that (and only that) phenomenon. Furthermore, the conditions to which it applies should be clearly spelled out. Therefore, the conditions should apply specifically to a given situation.

What Is the Grounded Theory Approach?

The grounded theory approach is a qualitative research **method** that uses a **systematic** set of **procedures** to **develop** an inductively derived grounded **theory** about a **phenomenon**. The research findings constitute a theoretical formulation of the reality under investigation, rather than consisting of a set of numbers, or a group of loosely related themes. Through this methodology, the concepts and relationships among them are not only generated but they are also provisionally tested. The procedures of the approach are many and rather specific, as you will see.

The purpose of grounded theory method is, of course, to build theory that is faithful to and illuminates the area under study. Researchers working in this tradition also hope that their theories will ultimately be related to others within their respective disciplines in a cumulative fashion, and that the theory's implications will have useful application.

Where Did the Grounded Theory Approach Originate?

Grounded theory as a methodology was originally developed by two sociologists: Barney Glaser and Anselm Strauss. While each came from different philosophic and research backgrounds their respective contributions were equally important. They worked in very close collaboration to develop the techniques for analyzing qualitative data that reflect both of their educations and backgrounds.

Anselm Strauss came from the University of Chicago, which had a long history and strong tradition in qualitative research. While there, he was also influenced by Interactionist and Pragmatist writings. Thus his thinking was inspired by men such as Robert E. Park, W. I. Thomas, John Dewey, G. H. Mead, Everett Hughes, and Herbert Blumer. What this background contributed to the method, among other things, were: (a) the need to get out into the field, if one wants to understand what is going on; (b) the importance of theory, grounded in reality, to the development of a discipline; (c) the nature of experience and undergoing as continually evolving; (d) the active role of persons in shaping the worlds they live in; (e) an emphasis on change and process, and the variability and complexity of life; and (f) the interrelationships among conditions, meaning, and action. Strauss also had prior actual experience in field research and had thought a lot about the subtle interplay of data collection and analysis and a few of the coding procedures that would later be elaborated (Strauss et al., 1964).

Barney Glaser came from a very different tradition but with some important shared features that no doubt permitted the collaboration of the two men. He received his training at Columbia University and was influenced by Paul Lazarsfeld, known as an innovator of quantitative methods. Later while doing qualitative analysis, Glaser especially saw the need for a well thought out, explicitly formulated, and systematic set of procedures for both coding and testing hypotheses generated during the research process. The Columbia tradition also emphasized empirical research in conjunction with the development of theory. Both the Chicago and the Columbia research traditions were directed at producing research that would be of use to professional or lay audiences. For this reason, much of the grounded theory writing that emerged from the Glaser-Strauss collaboration, including the original monographs about dying (1965, 1968), were addressed to those audiences as well as to their disciplinary colleagues.

What Are the Requisites for Learning This Approach?

As with any skill, proficiency in doing grounded theory comes with continued study and practice. In time, almost anyone who so desires should be able to reach sufficient level of skill and ease to do effective and useful research providing the following conditions are met.

(1) One must **study**, not merely read, through the procedures as described in the various books and be prepared to follow them (Glaser, 1978; Glaser & Strauss, 1967; Strauss, 1987). The procedures are designed to systematically and carefully build theory. Taking shortcuts in the work will result in a poorly constructed and narrowly conceived theory that may not be an accurate representation of reality.

(2) The procedures must be followed in doing research. In other words to take a class on grounded theory does not make one a grounded theorist. It is only by **practicing the procedures** through continued research that one gains sufficient understanding of how they work, and the skill and experience that enables one to continue using the techniques with success.

(3) A certain amount of **openness** and **flexibility** are necessary in order to be able to adapt the procedures to different phenomenon and research situations.

Is Grounded Theory Only a Sociological Approach?

Grounded theory can be used successfully by persons of many disciplines. One need not be a sociologist or subscribe to the Interactionist perspective to use it. What counts are the procedures and they are not discipline bound. It is important to remember that investigators from different disciplines will be interested in different phenomena—or may even view the same phenomenon differently because of disciplinary perspectives and interests. For example, take an area of study like children in a grade school. A nurse might be interested in their health problems, but a psychologist their adjustments, a sociologist group behavior, an educator in the students' learning process and patterns, and a phenomenologist (from any discipline) in their school experiences. Each perspective colors the approach taken to the study of these children. Yet, the grounded theory approach can provide each investigator with procedures for analyzing data that will lead to the development of theory useful to that discipline. A multidisciplinary study could also be done using grounded procedures, with each researcher bringing his or her special outlook and contribution to the research endeavor. Any theory that eventually evolves would reflect their respective perspectives.

Is Grounded Theory a "Scientific Method"? If so, Where Does Creativity Fit In?

Yes, grounded theory is a scientific method. Its procedures are designed so that, if they are carefully carried out, the method meets the criteria for doing "good" science: significance, theory-observation compatibility, generalizability, reproducibility, precision, rigor, and verification. (These are discussed further in Chapter 14. See also Corbin & Strauss, 1990, for a more in-depth discussion on the topic.)

The issue here is not whether the canons are met, but how they are **interpreted** and **defined** in the grounded theory approach. The canons represent only the most general of specific guidelines, and qualitative researchers run the danger of interpreting them too specifically in terms of the more positivistic interpretations developed by quantitative researchers. The proponents of each mode of discovery should, in fact, evolve more specific standards, based on particular procedures they have found useful in their investigations.

Creativity is also a vital component of the grounded theory method. Its procedures force the researcher to break through assumptions and to create new order out of the old. Creativity manifests itself in the ability of the researcher to aptly name categories; and also to let the mind wander and make the free associations that are necessary for generating stimulating questions, and for coming up with the comparisons that led to discovery. The comparisons sensitize the researcher, as we shall see later, enabling him or her to recognize potential categories, and identify relevant conditions and consequences when they appear in the data. While creativity is necessary to develop an effective theory, of course, the researcher must always validate any categories and statements of relationships arrived at creatively through the total research process.

How Are Discoveries Made?

Apropos of creativity, the early days of a research project can be a complex time for a beginning qualitative researcher. There is the excitement of making the first interviews or spending the first days in the field. There can also be some frustration engendered by the slow pace of getting started on one's research, either because of delay in gaining access to sources of data or obtaining necessary permission from a human-consent committee. Once past those initial difficulties, many researchers find the data collection deeply satisfying. Yet, the most gratifying moments of research for analytically inclined researchers will be those that bear on their discoveries. They may be matters of quick flashes of "intuition," or major breakthroughs in understanding the meanings and patterns of events, or the deeper satisfaction of having solved the research's major puzzles—or even just the more ordinary but still exciting nailing down of a less earth shattering analytic point.

Where do such discoveries come from? **Where** they come from is commonly confused with where the researcher happens to be **when** they come. A brief story will clarify this point. When the first book about grounded theory was about to go to a publisher, a draft of it was sent to an anthropologist friend who apparently only scanned it before sending a one-page letter of thanks. However, he also remonstrated: Why write a book about this? After all, ideas come from everywhere—whether when stepping off of street cars or somewhere else. Of course that is true; however, ideas don't come to everyone and about everything. Only under certain conditions will those insights arise. To begin with, the researcher has to be thinking about data—preferably be steeped in them, know a lot about the area under study. At the same time, he or she has to be puzzled or disturbed about some feature of those data or about their interpretations, so that questions and answers will be raised and sought. These are raised and sought even if on a subliminal level of consciousness, and sometimes for quite a time, before the vital question or answer breaks through to consciousness. Although knowledgeable about data and theory, the investigator somehow has to escape the very features of his or her work that may otherwise block the new perspective inherent in the sudden hunch, the flash of insight, the brilliant idea, or the profoundly different theoretical formulation. Specific knowledge, alas, is not only necessary but at times constitutes mental baggage that impedes this kind of intellectual creativity. In fact, many scientists are outstanding experts in their specialties, and even competent researchers, but are not particularly creative.

What Is the Difference Between Theory and Description?

This question is often asked by beginning researchers. Basically, the answer comes down to two main points. First, theory uses **concepts**. Similar data are grouped and given conceptual labels. This means placing interpretations on the data. Second, the concepts are related by means of **statements of relationship**. In description, data may be organized according to themes. These themes may be conceptualizations of data, but are more likely to be a précis or summaries of words taken directly from the data. There is **little, if any, interpretation** of data. Nor is there any attempt to relate the themes to form a conceptual scheme.

Is It Necessary to Transcribe
All of Your Interviews or Fieldnotes?

The general rule of thumb here is to transcribe only as much as is needed. But that is not necessarily an easy decision to make, nor can it be made sensibly until you are well into the course of the study itself. "Only as much as is needed," and some of the advice given below, should **not** be read as giving license to transcribe just a few of your first interviews or your taped fieldnotes. And indeed, if either this is your first study, and you are still quite inexperienced in this kind of research, or you are doing such a small scale study and have relatively few interviews or fieldnotes, then it is wiser to transcribe all of those materials.

There may or may not be the need—for your particular research purposes—to transcribe all of your taped materials; or indeed every paragraph or line of each interview or taped fieldnote. The actual transcribing (which can involve considerable time, energy, and money) should be **selective**. The mode of operation in the grounded theory style of analysis is generally as follows. The very first interviews or fieldnotes should be entirely transcribed and analyzed before going on to the next interviews or field observations. This early coding gives guidance to the next field observations and/or interviews, as will be described later in the book.

Later, as your theory develops, you may wish to listen to the tapes and transcribe only those sentences, passages, or paragraphs that relate to your evolving theory. (Early in the study, one is not certain what pertains and what does not, so it is better to transcribe everything, otherwise important data might be missed.) Transcribing those selected portions of material will not necessarily relieve you later of further transcribing, should you need to do additional or more detailed analysis, however. The bottom line is that the theory should guide not only what you look for and where you go to find it in the field, but also what you look for in your data. This leaves open the possibility that you may collect data, especially near the end of your study when your analysis tells you there is a hole in your theoretical formulations that needs closing and that further data collection is needed to close it. Then, you may want to transcribe only those portions of the interviews or fieldnotes that pertain to the theoretical gap that sent you back to the field.

In the end, it is you who must decide, unless a thesis committee or advisor insists otherwise, just how much of your interviews and fieldnotes to transcribe. You must determine what the purpose of your study is, what kind of additional analytic (theoretically sensitive as well as "psychologically" sensitive) contribution that given portions of transcribed versus untranscribed materials are making to the total study. You may need nearly full transcription in order to obtain the density of theory you desire. You may also want full transcription if you have the money to pay someone else to transcribe the tapes.

Regardless of whether you transcribe all or part of your tapes, it is still important to listen to the tapes. Listening as well as transcribing is essential for full and varied analysis. A final note: **better more than less.** But in the end, the final responsibility and the judgment are yours.

Summary

Grounded theory is a qualitative research approach that was collaboratively developed by Glaser and Strauss. Its systematic techniques and procedures of analysis enable the researcher to develop a substantive theory that meets the criteria for doing "good" science: significance, theory-observation compatibility, generalizability, reproducibility, precision, rigor, and verification. While the procedures are designed to give the analytic process precision and rigor, creativity is also an important element. For it is the latter that enables the researcher to ask pertinent questions of the data and to make the kind of comparisons that elicit from the data new insights into phenomenon and novel theoretical formulations. This approach can be used by persons of any discipline or theoretical orientation desirous of developing a grounded theory. However, careful **study** of the techniques and procedures outlined in this book and **practice** in their use are required to develop proficiency in the method.

2

Getting Started

One of the most difficult parts of doing research is to get started. The two major questions that seem most troublesome are: (a) How do I find a *researchable problem*? (b) How do I *narrow* it down sufficiently to make it workable? These questions may seem especially difficult if you are a novice at qualitative research because, at first glance, the process of making choices and commitments seems less well structured and more ambiguous than in quantitative forms of research. Our answers to these two questions will be framed within the context of the grounded theory method. The purpose of this chapter is to clarify some of the basic underlying principles that lie behind the making of those initial choices.

Research Problems

The sources of research problems in the grounded theory approach are no different from those of other approaches to qualitative research.

Sources of the Research Problem

There are several sources of researchable problems.

(1) *The suggested or assigned research problem.* One way to arrive at a problem is to ask for suggestions from a professor doing research in an area of interest. Often he or she has ongoing research projects and would welcome a graduate student taking on a small part of the project. This way of finding a problem tends to increase the possibility of getting involved in a "doable" and "relevant" research problem. This is because the more experienced researcher already knows what has been done and needs to be done in that particular substantive area. On the other hand, a choice arrived at in this manner may not be the most interesting to you. It is important to remember that whatever problem is selected, you will have to live with it for quite a while, so the final choice should be something that engages your interest.

A variant on this method is to follow up on a professional or collegial remark that an inquiry into such and such would be useful and interesting. This is often a more palatable source of a research problem, especially if you have some inclination toward that substantive area. For example, the interest of a woman who is athletic might be sparked by a remark such as: How do women who go to gyms feel about their bodies? This broad and open statement can lead to all sorts of questions. For example, do women who go to gymnasiums feel differently about their bodies than women who do not? Or, do women weight lifters feel differently about their bodies than women runners or men weight lifters?

Yet another variation of the "suggested research problem" is when a student is told that funding is available for research on certain topics. In fact, faculty sponsors may steer students in directions where funds are available. This is quite a legitimate suggestion, as often those are problem areas of special need.

(2) *The technical literature.* This can be a stimulus to research in several ways. Sometimes it points to a relatively unexplored area or suggests a topic in need of further development. At other times there are contradictions or ambiguities among the accumulated studies and writings. The discrepancies suggest the need for a study that will help to resolve those uncertainties. Alternatively, a researcher's reading on a subject may suggest that a new approach is needed to solve an old problem even though it has been well studied in the past. Something about the problem area and the phenomena associated with it remains elusive, and that something, if discovered, might be used to reconstruct understanding of this phenomenon. Also, while reading the literature you might be struck by a finding that is dissonant with your own experience, which can lead to a study resolving that dissonance. Finally, reading may simply stimulate curiosity about a subject. The minute one asks the question, "but what if" and finds there is no answer, then one has a problem area. (See Chapter 3 for further discussion of the uses of literature.)

(3) *Personal and professional experience.* These are often the sources of problems. A person may undergo a divorce and wonder how other women or men experienced their own divorces. Or, someone may come across a problem in his or her profession or workplace for which there is no known answer. Professional experience frequently leads to the judgment that some feature of the profession or its practice is less than effective, efficient, human, or equitable. So, it is believed, perhaps a good research study might help to correct that situation. Some professionals return to study for their higher degrees because they are motivated by that reform ambition. The research problems that they choose are grounded in that motivation.

Choosing a research problem through the professional or personal experience route may seem more hazardous than through the suggested or literature routes. This is not necessarily true.

The touchstone of your own experience may be more valuable an indicator for you of a potentially successful research endeavor.

Certainly, anyone who is curious or concerned about the world around himself or herself and who is willing to take risks should not, after some deliberation and using the sources suggested above, have too much trouble finding a problem area to study. The next step is asking the proper research question.

The Research Question

The way that one asks the research question is extremely important because that determines to a larger extent the research method that is used. Herein lies a dilemma. Does one choose the grounded theory method because the problem area and question stemming from it suggest that this method be used? Or, does one decide to use grounded theory methodology first and then frame the question to fit it?

Those issues are difficult to respond to because their answers are not cut and dry. Although the basic premise is that the research question should dictate the method, many persons are oriented toward quantitative research. So, even when the problem area suggests that a qualitative study is indicated, they will frame their questions in such a manner that these lead to a quantitative study. Other researchers, because of personal orientations, training, or convictions, tend to see problems from a qualitative perspective. The questions they ask about any problem area are couched in qualitative terms because they just don't see problems any other way. There is no reason for us to discuss this point here; we only want to note that some problem areas clearly suggest one form of research over another and that an investigator should be true to the problem at hand. For instance, if someone wanted to know whether one drug is more effective than another, then a double blind clinical trial would be more appropriate than a grounded theory study.

However, if someone wanted to know what it was like to be a participant in a drug study, then he or she might sensibly engage in a grounded theory project or some other type of qualitative study. Clearly, preference and training play a part in these decisions, but these should not blind us to other methodological options.

Another important aspect of the research question is the setting of boundaries on what will be studied. It is impossible for any investigator to cover all aspects of a problem. The research question helps to narrow down the problem to a workable size. (This is the second major question mentioned previously as confronting researchers, especially inexperienced ones.)

Asking the Research Question

What then do grounded theory study questions look like? How do they differ from those of quantitative studies, and why?

Recall that the main purpose of using the grounded theory method is to develop theory. To do this, we need a research question or questions that will give us the flexibility and freedom to explore a phenomenon in depth. Also underlying this approach to qualitative research is the assumption that all of the concepts pertaining to a given phenomenon have not yet been identified, at least not in this population or place; or if so, then the relationships between the concepts are poorly understood or conceptually undeveloped. Or, perhaps there is the assumption that someone has never asked this particular research question in quite the same way, so it is as yet impossible to determine which variables pertain to this area and which do not. This reasoning creates the need for asking a type of question that will enable us to find answers to issues that seem important but remain unanswered.

While the initial question starts out broadly, it becomes progressively narrowed and more focused during the research process, as concepts and their relationships are discovered to be relevant or irrelevant. So, the research question begins as an open and broad one; but not so open, of course, as to allow for the entire universe of possibilities. Yet not so narrow and focused that it excludes discovery, which after all is the central purpose of using the grounded theory method. This endeavor does not entail statements about relationships between a dependent and an independent variable, as is common in quantitative studies, because we are not testing this kind of hypothesis. **The research question in a grounded theory study is a statement that identifies the phenomenon to be studied**. It tells you what you specifically want to focus on and what you want to know about this subject. Grounded theory questions also tend to be oriented toward **action** and **process**.

> *Note.* Here is an example of how one might write a grounded theory question.
>
> How do women manage a pregnancy complicated by a chronic illness? This question, at least in such global form, while too broad and unstructured for a quantitative study is a perfectly good one for a grounded theory study. The question tells you that the study will investigate women during pregnancy, and that the pregnancy will be complicated by a chronic illness. Furthermore, the study will be looking at management of the pregnancy from the womens' perspective; that is, what they do and think, not what the doctors, or someone else, do or think. Of course in a grounded theory study it is important also to investigate what the doctors do and what they tell the women, because these actions may influence how women manage their pregnancies but this is not the main issue. Determining how and to what extent womens' actions are influenced by others is only part of what the researcher wants to find out. The focus of the study is on **the women**, and keeping that in mind prevents the researcher from getting side tracked—and fumbling "all over the place."

Also, in terms of narrowing and focusing the problem, depending upon how the question is asked, the investigation can go in different directions or get focused on different things. For instance, if the investigator asks:

(1) What happens when a patient complains of being in pain but the nurse doesn't believe him or her? In this case the investigator is asking an **interactional** question. Thus the focus of the observations, chart reviews and interviews, as well as the analysis, will be on interaction.

(2) What are the organizational mechanisms or policies for handling addictive drugs? In this case, the researcher is asking an **organizational** question, and will focus on the broader organizational responses to this drug problem. Data will be gathered not only through interviews but also by studying written policies, then observing how these are carried out. Not all organizational policies will be studied, rather only those related to the handling of addictive drugs.

(3) What difference does it make to patients' responses to pain medication that they have had long experience (at least two years) with pain and medication? Here a **biographical** question is being asked. Not only will the focus be on present responses to pain medication, but this will be examined in light of oral histories that shed light on past experiences with pain and its treatment.

Summary

The original research question is a directive that leads the researcher immediately to examine a specific performance, the site where events are occurring, documents, people acting, or informants to interview. It gets the researcher started and helps him or her to stay focused throughout the research project. Whenever he or she begins to flounder or get lost in the masses of data, the original question can always be returned to for clarification. Then, through analysis of the data, which begins with the first collection of data (the first interview or observation), the process of refining and specifying the question will begin. How this happens will be explained in the chapters on coding.

3

Theoretical Sensitivity

Theoretical sensitivity is a term frequently associated with grounded theory. It is in fact, the title of the book written on this method by Glaser (1978). But, just what is theoretical sensitivity? Where does it come from? How do we use it to aid rather than let it block our theory development? This chapter will explore these questions in a general sense, to provide background for more in-depth discussions that will follow in subsequent chapters. (For further reading on this subject, see Glaser, 1978, Chapter 1, and Glaser & Strauss, 1967, Chapter 9.)

Definition

Theoretical sensitivity refers to a personal quality of the researcher. It indicates an awareness of the subtleties of meaning of data. One can come to the research situation with varying degrees of sensitivity depending upon previous reading and experience with or relevant to an area. It can also be developed further during the research process. Theoretical sensitivity refers to the attribute of having insight, the ability to give meaning to data, the capacity to understand, and capability to separate the pertinent from that which isn't. All this is done in conceptual rather than concrete terms. It is theoretical sensitivity that allows one to develop a theory that is grounded, conceptually dense, and well integrated—and to do this more quickly than if this sensitivity were lacking.

Sources of Theoretical Sensitivity

Theoretical sensitivity comes from a number of sources. One source is **literature**, which includes readings on theory, research, and documents (e.g., biographies, government publications) of various kinds. By having some familiarity with these publications, you have a rich background of information that "sensitizes" you to what is going on with the phenomenon you are studying. (Specific uses of literature in grounded theory will be discussed in the next chapter.)

Professional experience is another source of sensitivity, if a researcher is fortunate enough to have had this experience. Throughout years of practice in a field, one acquires an understanding of how things work in that field, and why, and what will happen there under certain conditions. This knowledge, even if implicit, is taken into the research situation and helps you to understand events and actions seen and heard, and to do so more quickly than if you did not bring this background into the research. For example, a nurse studying nurses' work in hospitals can move into the situation and gain insight more quickly than someone who has never studied hospitals. The more professional experience, the richer the knowledge base and insight available to draw upon in the research. On the other hand, this kind of experience can also block you from seeing things that have become routine or "obvious." (In Chapter 6, we discuss techniques for breaking through such blinders.)

Personal experience represents still another source of theoretical sensitivity. As an example, the experience of having gone through a divorce can make one sensitive to what it means to experience loss. The loss experienced through the death of a loved one is different from that of divorce. However, in a conceptual sense there are similarities as well as differences between the two loss experiences. By drawing upon the personal experience of divorce, the analyst can have a basis for making comparisons that in turn stimulate the generation of potentially relevant concepts and their relationships that pertain to loss through death. (We discuss the use of comparisons in Chapter 6.) In addition, after you have had further experience with research projects, this too becomes a useful aspect of your personal experience. However, you must be careful not to assume that everyone else's experience has been similar to yours. Indeed, later as you discover or think about such differences, these data will provide your analysis with some variation.

Up to this point, we have been speaking about theoretical sensitivity as derived from the background that the analyst brings to the research situation. In addition, the **analytic process** itself provides an additional source for theoretical sensitivity. Insight and understanding about a phenomenon increase as you interact with your data. This comes from collecting and asking questions about the data, making comparisons, thinking about what you see, making hypotheses, developing small theoretical frameworks (miniframeworks) about concepts and their relationships. In turn, the researcher uses these to look again at the data. Often, one idea or insight sparks another, directing you to look more closely at the data, to give meaning to words that seemed previously not to have meaning, and to look for situations that might explain what is happening here. This increasing sensitivity to concepts, their meanings, and relationships is why it is so important to interweave data selection with data analysis. Each feeds into the other thereby increasing insight and recognition of the parameters of the evolving theory.

Keeping a Balance Between Creativity and Science

Theoretical sensitivity represents an important creative aspect of grounded theory. This sensitivity represents an ability not only to use personal and professional experience imaginatively, but also literature. It enables the analyst to see the research situation and its associated data in new ways, and to explore the data's potential for developing theory. As a famous biologist once wrote: "It is not to see something first, but to establish solid connections between the previously known and the hitherto unknown that constitutes the essence of specific discovery" (Selye, 1956, p. 6).

But Selye also added, the purpose for doing research is to build a theory that will contribute to the body of theoretical knowledge called science. So how can we be scientific and creative at the same time? How are we to become sufficiently free of biases and unrecognized or unexplored assumptions to produce a valid and reliable theory?

Admittedly, it is not easy to make creative use of one's knowledge and experience while at the same time holding on to the reality of a phenomenon rather than just thinking imaginatively about it. To assist you, we offer the following suggestions.

(1) **Periodically step back and ask**: What is going on here? Does what I think I see fit the reality of the data? The data themselves do not lie. How this difficult lesson was learned by one of the authors (Corbin) is described below.

While doing a study regarding the processes by which women with chronic illness managed their pregnancies, it quickly became evident that their actions were aimed at controlling risks associated with such a pregnancy, so that they might have a healthy baby. Furthermore, it was noticed that the risks varied over the course of the pregnancy, some of the time the risks were higher, other times they were lower. One would expect then that the management tactics would vary with the risks: the higher the risks, the more controlling the strategies. The researcher assumed that verifying this hypothesis would simply be a matter of checking it out against each case. Wrong!

What the researcher found was that sometimes the hypothesis was supported but sometimes it wasn't, much to her frustration. Try as she would, she could not force this hypothesis upon the data. It wouldn't work. Why not? Because, she was categorizing the pregnant women in terms of risk levels according to her own perception of the situation. This, as it turned out, was not necessarily their perception. In other words, the researcher "bought" the medical model of risk levels, but the pregnant women did not necessarily do so. Once the researcher went back to the data, questioned them and asked why particular statements and actions didn't fit her perceptions, she was able to identify that the women acted on the basis of their own perceptions of the situation. In other words, the risks that they assessed and balanced were not necessarily the same as those of health professionals. Once the original hypothesis was revised to reflect the reality of the situation, it fit all of the data. The women's own assessment and balancing of the risks influenced the numbers and types of strategies taken to control them.

(2) **Maintain an attitude of skepticism.** All theoretical explanations, categories, hypotheses, and questions about the data, whether they come directly or indirectly from the making of comparisons, the literature, or from experience, should be regarded as **provisional**. They always need to be checked out, played against the actual data, and never accepted as fact. For example, categories derived from the research literature (variables identified in previous studies) are always context specific. They may fit the study from whence they came. However, this does not necessarily mean that they apply to the situation you are studying, or come together with other concepts in quite the same way as in previous theories. Remember then, any theoretical explanations or categories brought to the research situation are considered provisional until supported by actual data (are found to fit this situation).

(3) **Follow the research procedures.** The data collection and analytic procedures are designed to give rigor to a study. At the same time they help you to break through biases, and lead you

to examine at least some of your assumptions that might otherwise affect an unrealistic reading of the data. There is a reason for alternating between collecting and analyzing data. Not only does this allow sampling on the basis of concepts emerging as relevant to that particular research situation, but it furthers verification of hypotheses while they are being developed. Those found invalid can then be revised to fit the reality of the situation under study. Coding is a systematic and precise set of procedures that can't be done haphazardly or at the whim of the researcher. (See Chapters 5, 6, 7, and 8.) In order for the emerging theory to be grounded, as well as valid and reliable, the procedures must be followed just as carefully as those that govern good quantitative studies. There are no double standards for one form of research over another. The procedures are different but the basic standards remain the same.

We would like to end our discussion on theoretical sensitivity with a quote from a book titled *Science: Methods and Meaning* (Rapport & Wright, 1964). In their introduction to the section on discovery the authors write:

> But chance is never the predominant factor in discovery. The beginning scientist who hopes by luck to emulate Lavoisier or Faraday, or even lesser scientists is directed to Pasteur's famous statement that "chance favors only the prepared mind." (pp. 130-131)

Summary

Theoretical sensitivity is the ability to recognize what is important in data and to give it meaning. It helps to formulate theory that is faithful to the reality of the phenomena under study (Glaser, 1978). Theoretical sensitivity has two sources. First, it comes from being well grounded in the technical literature as well as from professional and personal experience. You bring this complex knowledge into the research situation. However, theoretical sensitivity is also acquired during the research process through continual interactions with the data—through your collection and analyses of the data. While many of the analytic techniques that one uses to develop theoretical sensitivity are creative and imaginative in character, it is important to keep a balance between that which is created by the researcher and the real. You can do so by: (a) asking, what is really going on here?; (b) maintaining an attitude of skepticism toward any categories or hypotheses brought to or arising early in the research, and validating them repeatedly with the data themselves; and (c) by following the data collection and analytic procedures as discussed in this book. Good science (good theory) is produced through this interplay of creativeness and the skills acquired through training.

The Uses of Literature

Definition of Terms

Technical Literature: Reports of research studies, and theoretical or philosophical papers characteristic of professional and disciplinary writing. These can serve as background materials against which one compares findings from actual data gathered in grounded theory studies.

Nontechnical Literature: Biographies, diaries, documents, manuscripts, records, reports, catalogues, and other materials that can be used as primary data or to supplement interviews and field observations in grounded theory studies.

The literature, both technical and nontechnical, plays such an important and varied role in grounded theory that we would like to devote a few pages to exploring its uses. We'll begin first with the technical literature, then move on to the nontechnical.

Uses of the Technical Literature

We all bring to the inquiry a considerable background in professional and disciplinary literature (as mentioned in the previous chapter). We may have acquired this background while studying for examinations or simply through efforts to keep up with the literature in our field. To understand something of how and why we use the technical literature as we do in grounded theory, it is important to understand something of the logic underlying the method and to contrast this to the use of literature in quantitative methods.

For investigators using quantitative methods, the literature has very specific uses. It enables the user to identify previous research in an area, as well as to discover where there are gaps in understanding. It also suggests theoretical and conceptual frameworks that might be used to guide quantitative research projects and to interpret their findings. Then, too, the technical literature helps the researcher to delineate important variables for study and suggests relationships among them. All of these uses are important in quantitative studies because, for the most part, investigators are concerned with testing the relationships among variables, or determining how they cluster. They must know before beginning a study what the variables of interest are, then know how to interpret the findings arrived at through standard modes of testing.

In contrast, with grounded theory research, rather than testing the relationships among variables, we want to discover relevant categories and the relationships among them; to put together categories in new, rather than standard ways. So, if you begin with a list of already identified variables (categories), they may—and are indeed very likely to—get in the way of discovery. Also, in grounded theory studies, you want to explain phenomena in light of the theoretical framework that evolves during the research itself; thus, you do not want to be constrained by having to adhere to a previously developed theory that may or may not apply to the area under investigation. (If you carry within you **unrecognized assumptions** associated with a previously developed theory, you should become alert to some of these and how they affect your analysis, through the use of the techniques discussed in Chapter 6.)

If, after completing your study, you find that your emergent theory has some relationship to already recognized and developed theory, then you may want to use yours to extend the other. However, it is important to understand (as we note below) that as your theory evolves, you can incorporate seemingly relevant elements of previous theories, but only as they prove themselves to be pertinent to the data gathered in your study. Given what we have just explained, it makes no sense to start with "received" theories or variables (categories) because these are likely to inhibit or impede the development of new theoretical formulations, unless of course your purpose is to open these up and to find new meanings in them.

In summary, what we are saying is the following. You will come to the research situation with some background in the technical literature and it is important to acknowledge and use that, as we will explain below. However, there is no need to review all of the literature beforehand (as is frequently done by researchers trained in other approaches), because if we are effective in our analysis, then new categories will emerge that neither we, nor anyone else, had thought about previously. We do not want to be so steeped in the literature as to be constrained and even stifled in terms of creative efforts by our knowledge of it! Since discovery is our purpose, we do not have beforehand knowledge of all the categories relevant to our theory. It is **only** after a category has emerged as pertinent that we might want to go back to the technical literature to determine if this category is there, and if so what other researchers have said about it.

How Do We Use the Technical Literature?

The technical literature has various uses in grounded theory research. These are described below.

(1) **The literature can be used to stimulate theoretical sensitivity** by providing concepts and relationships that are checked out against actual data. Though you do not want to enter the field with an entire list of concepts and relationships, some may turn up over and over again in the literature and thus

appear to be significant. These you may want to bring to the field where you will look for evidence of whether or not the concepts and relationships apply to the situation that you are studying, and if so what form they take here.

There is a special sense in which published descriptive materials can be used to enhance theoretical sensitivity. These writings often give very accurate **descriptions** of reality, with very little interpretation other than, perhaps, organizing sections of materials according to a few themes. Reading them can make us sensitive for what to look for in our own data and help us to generate questions that we might want to ask our respondents. Also any **concepts** that come out of these studies may have relevance to our own. Here, too, we must be very careful to look for evidence in our data and to delineate the forms that they take in our study.

Knowledge of philosophic writings and existing theories can also provide ways of approaching and interpreting data. For instance, a researcher steeped in the perspective of Symbolic Interactionism might examine the meanings given to situations by the people involved. A Marxist might seek to determine the structure of economic exploitation in a situation.

If one is interested in extending an already existing theory, then one might begin with the existing theory and attempt to uncover how it applies to new and varied situations, as differentiated from those situations to which it was originally applied. For example, someone might wish to begin with the Awareness Context (Glaser & Strauss, 1965). This theory has to do with the keeping of secrets and evolved from Glaser and Strauss' studies on dying. A researcher wishing to extend this theory could apply the general framework of Awareness Context to situations of study such as: spies, marital infidelities, and gay and lesbian identities. The framework of Glaser and Strauss would provide a set of sensitizing concepts and relationships, which the researcher would verify against the data gathered in his or her study. With the findings from the second, the original theory could then be amended, added to, or modified to fit those particular situations.

(2) **The literature can be used as secondary sources of data**. Research publications often include quoted materials from interviews and fieldnotes, and these **quotations** can be used as secondary sources of data for your own purposes. The publications may also include **descriptive** materials concerning events, actions, setting, and actors' perspectives, that can be used as data and analyzed using the methods described in the following chapters. In fact, one form of qualitative research is the analysis of theoretical or philosophical statements and writing per se.

(3) **It can stimulate questions**. You can use the literature to derive a list of questions that you want to ask of your respondents or that guide your initial observations. This list (as we have said in Chapter 2) may change after the first interviews or observations, but it can help to get you started on your research and to satisfy school and human subject committees regarding your research intent. It can also be used to stimulate questions during the analysis process. For example, when there is a discrepancy between your data and the findings reported in the literature, that difference should send you back to the field or to your data to ask, "why the discrepancy? Am I overlooking something important? Are conditions different here? To what specific conditions can the differences be attributed?"

(4) **It can direct theoretical sampling**. The literature can give you ideas about where you might go to uncover phenomena important to the development of your theory. In other words, it can direct you to situations that you may not otherwise have thought of, but that are similar or different from those being studied; thereby enabling you to add variation to the study.

(5) **It can be used as supplementary validation**. When you have finished developing your theory and are writing up your findings, you can reference the literature in appropriate places to give validation of the accuracy of your findings. Or, you might want to point out how yours differs from the published literature and why. (You should be able to show what set of conditions were specifically operating in your situation and

their impact on phenomena.) What you *don't* want to do is constantly run back to the published literature to find validation for everything that you are seeing. This would hinder progress and stifle creativity.

An Example of How the
Technical Literature Can Be Used

The following is a memo mainly about technical-professional and disciplinary literature written by one of the authors (Corbin) after a group meeting on grounded theory. The memo brings out many of the features discussed above. The study discussed in the memo is that of a graduate student examining the experience of having cancer.

> G., a graduate student in sociology, came to the meeting saying that she wanted to do a grounded theory study on her literature. She says that she reviewed the literature on the basis of her interviews. The interviews gave her direction as to what literature she would go to next. In that sense, the readings are truly grounded in her study. For example, when someone that she interviewed talked about a particular type of medical treatment, then G. read up about that treatment. If they told her that they tried a nonmedical type of treatment like the Symington Method, she read about that too. By doing this, she found that there were different classes of readings: those that were strictly medical, biographies that described the experience, and those that talked about alternative forms of treatment.
>
> I was very intrigued with the problem G. presented. I couldn't see our doing a grounded theory just on the literature per se, because I felt that it is the interplay between data and literature that is important in this case. This is not a study of the literature but of people's experience with cancer. After listening to her, though, several things struck me about how she used the literature or could use it.
>
> The first thing that struck me was that there was an important difference between cancer as a disease and cancer as an experience;

however, the two are much interrelated, and the literature supports this. Sensitized to this fact, one can then go back to the
field and to collect data to determine how literature and data
compare, plus learn something about the nature of the relationship between them. The literature also tells us something about
the conditions that affect the disease course and the cancer experience and how they affect each. One can again go back to the field
and look for these conditions and trace out how they affect the
disease course and experience. For example, she found that certain medications may help to control the course of the disease,
but at the same time they make one's hair fall out, feel nauseated,
and decrease appetite. This has to affect the person's experience
and how they view their cancer, as a disease, especially if they do
a comparison of (how they looked and felt) before and after
having chemotherapy or other treatments—radiation, surgery.
Choosing a treatment like Symington, either as an alternative or
in conjunction with medical care, can also affect the experience
as well as impact upon the course. Conversely, having a poor
experience with either traditional or alternative medicine can
lead a person to turn to one or the other, or simply drop both. So,
consequences of one treatment can feed into the experience of the
next. All of this is speculation based on the literature and has to
be checked out against actual data, which will not only verify this
hypothesis but also give the specifics of how it all works.

Using literature in this way is like theoretically sampling it on
the basis of interviews, then going back and theoretically sampling in reality as based on the literature. Thus, the literature
makes one theoretically sensitive to: (1) **conditions** that influence
the experiences; (2) **strategies** for dealing with the experience
(since medications make me ill, I will try the Gerson diet, or
some other treatment and forget about traditional medicine); and
(3) **consequences** of what the experience is like. (People doing
Symington who nevertheless develop metastasis are sometimes
told, or believe themselves, they didn't think positively enough.)
The literature also suggests the notion of **process** or change over
time, and **variation** in types of experiences depending upon the
choices the ill person makes. Finally, the literature directs us to
sample a variety of situations.

By choosing the right literature in tandem with doing analysis one can learn much about the broader and narrower conditions that influence a phenomenon. As Anselm Strauss says, "the library is like many voices talking to you. All you have to do is listen." **Of course, any categories, hypotheses, and so forth, generated by the literature have to be checked out against real (primary) data.** The interplay of reading the literature and doing an analysis of it, then moving out into the field to verify it against reality can yield an integrated picture and enhance the conceptual richness of the theory.

Nontechnical Literature

The nontechnical literature is comprised of letters, biographies, diaries, reports, videotapes, newspapers, and a variety of other materials. Though these are usually not used as sources of data in quantitative studies, they play an essential role in grounded theory studies. They can be used as primary data, especially in historical or biographical studies. In most studies they are important sources of data, supplementing the more usual interviews and observations. For example, much can be learned about an organization, its structure, and how it functions (that may not immediately be visible in observations or interviews) by studying its reports, correspondence, and memos.

The nontechnical literature can be used for all of the same purposes as the technical literature. However, there is one added feature. Since it is often difficult to authenticate and determine the veracity of some documents, biographies, and such, it is very important to cross-check these against other sources of data if possible, such as interview and observation. Or, if you are doing a life history study, you should read a wide variety of biographies and other documents such as letters and examine them closely for similarities and differences.

Summary

Each type of literature tends to be useful in somewhat different and specific ways, yielding diverse sorts of ranges of data (about personal histories or organizational events, for instance), or research findings, or theoretical formulations. Ingenious researchers, besides using the usual technical literature, will sometimes use various other types of published and unpublished materials to supplement their interviews and field observations.

All kinds of literature can be used before a research study is begun: both in thinking about and getting the study off the ground. They can also be used during the study itself, contributing to its forward thrust. In fact, there should also be some searching out of the literature (but not just technical) during the research itself, an actual interplay of reading literature and data analysis. So, in effect, we read and use published materials during all phases of the research. We remind you, however, that categories and their relationships must be checked against your primary data. You can use all types of literature judged as relevant, but must guard against becoming a captive of any of them.

Part II

Coding Procedures

We have now come to the heart of the book, the chapters on analysis, or coding as it is often called. Coding represents the operations by which data are broken down, conceptualized, and put back together in new ways. It is the central process by which theories are built from data.

What is so special about the coding process in developing a grounded theory? What makes it different from other methods of analysis? As we have said in the introductory chapters, its purposes are broader than enabling the researcher to pull out a few themes, or to develop a descriptive theoretical framework of loosely interwoven concepts. To summarize what we have said previously, the analytic procedures of grounded theory are designed to:

(1) Build rather than only test theory.
(2) Give the research process the rigor necessary to make the theory "good" science.
(3) Help the analyst to break through the biases and assumptions brought to, and that can develop during, the research process.
(4) Provide the grounding, build the density, and develop the sensitivity and integration needed to generate a rich, tightly woven, explanatory theory that closely approximates the reality it represents.

To reach these ends requires maintaining a balance among the attributes of creativity, rigor, persistence, and above all, theoretical sensitivity. This is a strange combination of qualities, we agree, but precisely those present whenever discoveries, great and small, are made. Though ordinarily a beginner cannot expect to make "great" discoveries, with enough hard work and persistence a researcher is capable of making contributions to his or her field of interest. What we intend to provide are a number of techniques to assist you, the analyst, to make use of **your creative capacities,** and to further develop the **theoretical sensitivity** that may be already **present within you.** It is up to you to provide the hard work.

Analysis in grounded theory is composed of three major types of coding. These are: (a) open coding; (b) axial coding; and (c) selective coding. Each will be described in the following chapters, along with chapters on techniques for enhancing theoretical sensitivity and discovering process in data. The final analytic chapter (Chapter 10) pulls all of the analysis chapters into a framework we call the *conditional matrix.* It is in effect an analytical framework for grounded theory.

Here we want to emphasize that the lines between each type of coding are artificial. The different types do not necessarily take place in stages. In a single coding session, you might quickly and without self-consciousness move between one form of coding and another, especially between open and axial coding. Though these two forms of coding are most likely to take place in the earlier phases of the project, they may also occur near the end. This is because during the selective coding, one almost always finds some concepts that remain poorly developed or unintegrated. At that time, however, both open and axial coding are done in the service of selective coding; they also "feel" different in this context.

The other major point to be made here is that data collection and data analysis are tightly interwoven processes, and must occur alternately because the analysis directs the sampling of data. (More will be said about this in Chapter 11 on Theoretical Sampling.) We will not emphasize the data collection process, per se, because this is so well discussed in the many excellent books available on doing fieldwork.

Before entering our discussion of coding, we would like to leave you with four important thoughts.

1. Doing analysis is, in fact, making interpretations and there is good reason for this. As Diesing (1971, p. 14), a philosopher of science, says:

> actually scientific knowledge is in large part an invention or development rather than an imitation; concepts, hypotheses, and theories are not found ready-made in reality but must be constructed.

2. The second is that while we set these procedures and techniques before you, we do *not* at all wish to imply rigid adherence to them. Again to quote Diesing (1971, p. 14):

> The procedures are not mechanical or automatic, nor do they constitute an algorithm guaranteed to give results. They are rather to be applied flexibly according to circumstances; their order may vary, and alternatives are available at every step.

3. In fact, one general technique that is central to all coding procedures and that helps to ensure your flexible use of those procedures is the **asking of questions**. You should be asking questions all along the course of your research project. As you read the next chapters, you will

see so many questions being asked about the phenomena under study, and about their various properties, dimensions, paradigm components, and so forth, that if for some reasons you wished to keep track of them you would be hard pressed to do so. This is because they are so numerous and so diverse. They are numerous because a genuinely creative researcher *must* ask questions. They are diverse, because each coding procedure in grounded theory methodology calls forth different kinds and ranges of questions. (You will be able to see this illustrated in the next chapters.) Since some procedures are more characteristic of earlier or later phases of a research project, the kinds of questions asked will also differ somewhat by research phase. So pay special attention to how these questions pepper the pages of these chapters, and practice asking these analystic questions yourself. Because they are **analytic** questions they are likely to be generative questions—that is, **generative** for the analysis itself.

4. We strongly recommend that after reading the chapters on coding (rapidly if you wish), that then you **study each in great detail**. These chapters (5-10) cover basic analytic procedures and their logic. Each procedure must be understood before proceeding to the next, otherwise your overall understanding of them will be less secure than you would wish. Once grasped, and **practiced** they become really effective research tools.

5

Open Coding
Definition of Terms

Concepts: Conceptual labels placed on discrete happenings, events, and other instances of phenomena.

Category: A classification of concepts. This classification is discovered when concepts are compared one against another and appear to pertain to a similar phenomenon. Thus the concepts are grouped together under a higher order, more abstract concept called a category.

Coding: The process of analyzing data.

Code Notes: The products of coding. These are one type of memo.

Open Coding: The process of breaking down, examining, comparing, conceptualizing, and categorizing data.

Properties: Attributes or characteristics pertaining to a category.

Dimensions: Location of properties along a continuum.

Dimensionalizing: The process of breaking a property down into its dimensions.

Science could not exist without *concepts*. Why are they so essential? Because by the very act of naming phenomena, we fix continuing attention on them. Once our attention is fixed, we can begin to examine and ask questions about those phenomena (now of course, labeled as concepts). Such questions not only describe what we see, but in the form of *propositions* (hypotheses) suggest how phenomena might possibly be related to one another. Propositions permit deductions, which in turn guide data collection that leads to further induction and provisional testing of propositions. In the end, communication among investigators, including the vital interplay of discussion and argument necessary to enhance the development of science, is made possible by the *specification of concepts and their relationships* phrased in terms of propositions. (These points are discussed in detail by Blumer, 1969, pp. 153-182.)

So what does all of the above have to do with *open coding*? Open coding is the part of analysis that pertains specifically to the naming and categorizing of phenomena through close examination of data. Without this first basic analytical step, the rest of the analysis and communication that follows could not take place. During open coding the data are broken down into discrete parts, closely examined, compared for similarities and differences, and questions are asked about the phenomena as reflected in the data. Through this process, one's own and others' assumptions about phenomena are questioned or explored, leading to new discoveries.

Procedures

Two analytic procedures are basic to the coding process, though their nature changes with each type of coding. The first pertains to the *making of comparisons*, the other to the *asking of questions*. In fact, grounded theory is often referred to in the literature as "the constant comparative method of analysis" (Glaser & Strauss, 1967, pp. 101-116). These two procedures help to give the concepts in grounded theory their precision and specificity. Let us show you how these two procedures are used to reach the goals of conceptualizing and categorizing data through open coding. These processes are not labeled as we go along. You have to watch closely to see how we use them. For more discussion on these techniques see Glaser (1978, pp. 56-72), Glaser and Strauss (1987, pp. 106-107), and Strauss (1987, pp. 58-64).

Labeling Phenomena

We have already remarked on why concepts are the basic units of analysis in the grounded theory method. One can count "raw" data, but one can't relate or talk about them easily. **Therefore, conceptualizing our data becomes the first step in analysis.** By breaking down and conceptualizing we mean taking apart an observation, a sentence, a paragraph, and giving each discrete incident, idea, or event, a name, something that stands for or represents a phenomenon. Just how do we do this? We ask questions about each one, like: What is this? What does it represent? We compare incident with incident as we go along so that similar phenomena can be given the same name. Otherwise, we would wind up with too many names and very confused!

Let's stop here and take an example. Suppose you are in a fairly expensive but popular restaurant. The restaurant is built on three levels. On the first level is a bar, on the second a small dining area, and on the third, the main dining area and the kitchen. The kitchen is open, so you can see what is going on. Wine, liqueurs, and appropriate glasses in which to serve them are also available on this third level. While waiting for your dinner, you notice a lady in red. She appears to be just standing there in the kitchen, but your common sense tells you that a restaurant wouldn't pay a lady in red just to stand there, especially in a busy kitchen. Your curiosity is piqued, so you decide to do an inductive analysis to see if you can determine just what her job is. (Once a grounded theorist, always a grounded theorist.)

You notice that she is intently looking around the kitchen area, **a work site**, focusing here and then there, taking a mental note of what is going on. *You ask yourself, what is she doing here? Then you label it* **watching**. Watching what? **Kitchen work**.

Next, someone comes up and asks her a question. She answers. This act is different than watching, so *you code it* as **information passing**.

She seems to notice everything. You call this **attentiveness**.

Our lady in red walks up to someone and tells him something. Since this incident also involves information that is passed on, *you also label it*, **information passing**.

Although standing in the midst of all this activity, she doesn't seem to disrupt it. *To describe this phenomenon* you use the term **unintrusiveness**.

She turns and walks quickly and quietly, **efficiency**, into the dining area, and proceeds to **watch**, the activity here also.

She seems to be keeping track of everyone and everything, **monitoring**. But monitoring what? Being an astute observer you notice that she is monitoring the **quality** of the service, how the waiter interacts and responds to the customer; the **timing of service**, how much transpires between seating a customer, their ordering, the delivery of food; and **customer response and satisfaction** with the service.

A waiter comes with an order for a large party, she moves in to help him, **providing assistance**.

The woman looks like she knows what she is doing and is competent at it, **experienced**.

She walks over to a wall near the kitchen and looks at what appears to be a schedule, **information gathering**.

The maitre d' comes down and they talk for a few moments and look around the room for empty tables and judge at what point in the meal the seated customers seem to be: the two are **conferring**.

This example should be sufficient for you to comprehend what we mean by labeling phenomena. It is not unusual for beginning researchers to summarize rather than *conceptualize* data. That is, they merely repeat briefly the gist of the phrase or sentence, but still in a descriptive way. For instance, instead of using a term such as "conferring" to describe the last incident, they might say something like "sat and talked to the maitre d'." Or, use terms such as: "read the schedule," "moved to the dining room," and "didn't disrupt." To invent such phrases doesn't give you a concept to work with. You can see just from this initial coding session that conceptually it is more effective to work with a term such as "information gathering" rather than "reading the schedule," because one might be able to label ten different happenings or events as **information gathering**—her asking a question of one of the chefs, checking on the number of clean glasses, calling a supplier, and so forth.

Discovering Categories

In the course of our research, we may come up with dozens, even hundreds of conceptual labels. (It is not unusual for beginning students to come into a teaching session with three to four typed pages of listed concepts.) These concepts also have to be grouped, like with like, otherwise we would wind up in a plight similar to that of the old lady in the shoe with so many children (concepts) we wouldn't know what to do (and that is exactly how students sometimes feel at this point).

Once we have identified particular phenomena in data, we can begin to group our concepts around them. This is done to reduce the number of units with which we have to work. The process of grouping concepts that seem to pertain to the same phenomena is called *categorizing*. (Notice here that we say "seem to." This is because at this point any proposed relationships are still considered provisional. We will talk more about this under Axial Coding in Chapter 7.) The phenomenon represented by a category is given a conceptual name, however this name should be more abstract than that given to the concepts grouped under it. Categories have conceptual power because they are able to pull together around them other groups of concepts or subcategories.

We still haven't answered our question about the nature of the job of our lady in red, so let us return to our example, and talk about categories at the same time. There are different ways to approach the categorization process. Thus we can take each concept as we go along with our labeling process, and ask to what class of phenomenon does it seem to pertain, and is it similar or different from the one before or after? Or, we can step back and look at the entire observation with many concepts in mind and say: What does this seem do be about? Using either method, we should reach the same conclusion. We shall illustrate the second approach only, our purpose not being to talk now about various ways of categorizing but to clarify *what* is entailed in the process of categorizing.

As an example, we might take the concept **monitoring** and ask: Why is she monitoring the traffic flow? the customer satisfaction? the quality of service? and the timing? Is it for the same or for a different purpose than the watching that she's doing in the kitchen? Or the conferring she is doing with the maitre d? What does being experienced have to do with the monitoring? Here we might conclude that monitoring, conferring, and watching all seem to pertain to the same thing—**work** that she is engaging in to **assess and maintain the flow of work**. It is a special kind of work however—preparing and bringing food to a table in a restaurant. We can label all concepts pertaining to work as: **types of work for assessing and maintaining work flow**. But, the concept **experience** doesn't quite fit under this heading. If we compare it with unintrusiveness and attentiveness, it is similar. Thus the three can be grouped under the heading of *attributes* or qualities. But attributes and qualities of what? Answer: A person good at assessing and maintaining the flow of work. But this long phrase is far too cumbersome, so we must give her job a better name. Since the job seems to have to do with keeping the flow of work going in a restaurant, and since the work pertains to food, we might call her a **food orchestrator**. Then, attentiveness, unintrusiveness, and experience become "attributes of" or "conditions" for a good restaurant food orchestrator. Attributes or conditions refer to a different, but related class of phenomena. So, we now have a category (Food Orchestrator) and two subcategories (Types of work for Assessing and Maintaining Work Flow; also Conditions for being a good Food Orchestrator). Remember that at the beginning of this chapter we gave a definition of "category." We suggest you go back and read it again in light of the preceding paragraphs.

Now the lady's actual job title will of course not be "restaurant food orchestrator" but that's close enough for us. She is no longer the mysterious lady in red. In our minds we have classified her by giving her a job title, and we know a little about her tasks and the attributes that it takes to do them. (Indeed, many a study has originated with just these kinds of casual observations or conversations, which become more serious, intense, and systematic when the observer or listener decides: "This is really worth studying, or at least could be great fun.") If we were doing a real grounded theory study, we couldn't stop here just with the initial observations and coding. (Although if your purpose is just to pull out themes, then you could pretty much stop here.) You want more than just a listing of concepts or even a grouping of them. Categories, after all, have to be analytically developed by the researcher. Before going on, though, we would like to momentarily take a look at how categories get their names.

Naming a Category

How do categories get named? In the example above, the name of the category "food orchestrator" was the investigator's own invention. This is where most names come from—YOU! The name you choose is usually the one that seems most logically related to the data it represents, and should be graphic enough to remind you quickly of its referent. But, it must be a more abstract concept than the ones it denotes. Don't feel overburdened with choosing the right name, at least not at first. Later, if you come up with a more appropriate name, you can change the original. *The important thing is to name a category,* so that you can remember it, think about it, and most of all begin to develop it analytically.

Some names will come from the pool of concepts that you already have from your disciplinary and professional reading. (See Chapter 4.) Before we discuss these kinds of literature-derived concepts, let us talk about your own concepts. As you are moving along in your coding, you might notice and name a phenomenon that is more abstract or that seems to incorporate other concepts. To illustrate: Suppose you were doing a study of children at play and had already coded your observations, using terms such as "grabbing," "hiding," "avoiding," and "discounting." You think then about the next incident and when you say "What is this, and to what phenomenon does it relate?" Then you respond with "a strategy to avoid sharing a toy." Here, you might say, "Oh, in fact, these are all strategies to avoid sharing a toy!" Thus you group the children's grabbing, hiding, avoiding, discounting, and anything else pertinent that comes along all under that one heading.

However, you can also borrow a name from the technical literature, terms such as: "caretaker fatigue," "illness experience," "status loss." Such concepts have some advantages insofar as they are loaded with analytic meaning and may already be considerably well developed in their own right. In using them, you may contribute beyond your own study to add to the development of concepts that are of importance and concern within your own discipline or profession.

On the other hand, we must remind you again that *use of borrowed concepts can have a grave disadvantage.* Borrowed concepts often bring with them commonly held meanings and associations. The concepts mentioned above, as well as others such as "stigma," "body image," and "cognitive dissonance," are perfectly good words. But the people reading your theory will expect you to define them in standard ways, or read these meanings into your work. You too can be biased by them and lay the standard meanings on top of your work, in essence stopping the inquiry in its tracks instead of opening it.

So while you may certainly use concepts from the literature, do so with care and be precise about your meanings.

Another important source of names are the words and phrases used by informants themselves, catchy ones that immediately draw your attention to them. These terms are called *"in vivo" codes* (Glaser, 1978, p. 70; Strauss, 1987, p. 33). Again we illustrate. The scene is a hospital unit, where we are doing a study of head nurses. While the head nurse and investigator are discussing the policies and procedures of the unit, the head nurse points to one of the LVNs (licensed vocational nurse) on the unit and says, "she is the tradition bearer of the unit." The head nurse goes on to explain that this particular LVN has taken on the responsibility of initiating all new employees to the traditions, rules, and policies of the unit. She also acts as rule enforcer reprimanding others whenever she notices that these are broken. Now the term "tradition bearer" is a great name for a category. It's catchy, suggesting and summarizing all the things that the head nurse said about this person. In using the term we not only have a good term but we will, as with all categories, then go on to develop that category, beginning by listing some of its properties. For example, the tradition bearer initiates new employees into the ward traditions, and is a prominent enforcer of the rules.

Developing Categories in Terms of Their Properties and Dimensions

When you begin to develop a category you do so first in terms of its *properties*, which can then be *dimensionalized*. Recall that in the definitions section of this chapter we said properties are the characteristics or attributes of a category, and that *dimensions* represent locations of a property along a continuum. The process of open coding stimulates the discovery not only of categories but also of their properties and dimensions.

Properties and dimensions are important to recognize and systematically develop because they form the basis for making relationships between categories and *subcategories*. And still later, between major categories. Therefore, to understand the nature of properties and dimensions and their relationships is a requisite task for understanding, in turn, all of the analytic procedures for developing a grounded theory.

As defined above, properties are attributes or characteristics of a phenomenon (category). Let us look at the category of "color." Its properties include: shade, intensity, hue, and so forth. Each of these properties can be dimensionalized; that is, they vary along continua. Thus color can vary in intensity from high to low; in hue from darker to lighter; and so forth.

The properties listed above are *general properties* of color. They can pertain to color regardless of the situation in which color is found. Knowing such general properties of a category is important because these give you the full range of dimensions over which a category might vary. Each time an instance of a category occurs in the data, it is possible to locate it somewhere along the *dimensional continua*. Therefore, each specific instance of the same general property (such as color) will have a different location on the dimensional continua. Hence, each category has several general properties, and each property varies over a dimensional continuum. In effect, this gives each occurrence of a category a separate *dimensional profile*. Several of these profiles can be grouped to give you a *pattern*. The dimensional profile represents the *specific properties* of a phenomenon under a given set of conditions.

As an example, think of the appearance of color in different types of flowers. Each time that a flower appears we can classify its color along the general properties mentioned earlier: shade, hue, and intensity. This is done in terms of where this flower is located along the dimensional continuum of each general property, thus giving the specific properties (or a color profile) for each flower. We can then group the flowers according to the specific profiles of color that they demonstrate, if we wish. This grouping will occur regardless of type of flower (whether pansies, peonies, or petunias). In one group we might have flowers showing dark hue, low intensity, or middle range of shade. Another group of flowers might show light hue, high intensity, and upper range of shade.

Any property of course will have subproperties. Each in turn can be dimensionalized, if analysis calls for it. For example, one property of flowers is its color. Color in turn will have many subproperties like hue, shade, intensity, and so forth. Another property of flowers is size. This, too, can be broken down into its subproperties like height, width, and thickness.

Let's go back to our original example—our lady in red—and apply to it what we've learned about properties and dimensions. In our first coding session we discovered the category **food orchestrator**. This category gives purpose and meaning to the presence in the restaurant of our lady in red, as opposed to say a restaurant patron who also may be wearing red. One of the subcategories of the category **food orchestrator** is that it requires performance of certain **types of work**, namely: watching, monitoring, assisting, and so forth. These latter are in fact a breakdown of the subcategory **types of work**. Now each of these types have properties that can be dimensionalized. With each incident of performance of a type of work we can give that incident specificity by looking at frequency of performance, duration, how it is carried out, who else is involved, when it is performed, and so forth.

Let us take the type of work called **watching**. With each incident of watching we can note its **frequency**. Frequency can be dimensionalized by asking: How often does she watch this area versus another, often—never? Watching also has the property of **extent**. Again with each incident we note, does she watch this one area more than another? Furthermore it has the property of **intensity**. Is the intensity with which she watches any area high or low and does this change over time? Another property is **duration** of watching. Does she watch an area a long or short time?

We can do the same with **information passing**. One property is **amount of information**. Does she pass a little or a lot of information with each incident of passing? Another is **manner of passing**. Is it done in writing or verbally, loudly or softly, overtly or covertly?

You can see how dimensionalizing enables us to give specificity to the work of our lady in red. If we were doing a study of restaurant food orchestrators, we would want this kind of specificity about each food orchestrator and each kind of work he or she does.

Graphically, properties and dimensions might be represented like this:

Category	Properties	Dimensional range
		(applied to each incident)
watching	frequency	often - - - - - - - - never
	extent	more - - - - - - - - less
	intensity	high - - - - - - - - low
	duration	long - - - - - - - - short

During analysis, properties are often found in their dimensional forms, or the specific properties pertaining to this instance of a phenomenon. These then point back to general properties. For instance, one might hear a student say "I spend all of my time studying." The word "all" is immediately a cue. It is a dimension of **time**, which is a general property or characteristic of studying that can vary from spending all to none of one's time studying. (If we wanted, we could become more specific and break time down into its subproperties, such as amount and type, and dimensionalize these also.)

Variations on Ways of Doing Open Coding

There are several different ways of approaching the process of open coding. One might begin by analyzing the first interview and observation with a **line-by-line analysis**. This involves close examination, phrase by phrase, and even sometimes of single words. This is perhaps the most detailed type of analysis, but the most generative. (It is also the most tedious if done for too many sessions. However, at the outset of a study, as well as when beginning to learn this coding procedure, using it can be very exciting just because it is so generative.) Generating your categories early through line-by-line analysis is important because categories also become the basis of your theoretical sampling. They tell you what to focus on in your next interview or observational site, and give you some idea of where you might go to find instances of the phenomenon to which the category refers. For example, line-by-line analysis may direct you to compare the first restaurant with a busy but not so well-to-do restaurant, where there might not be a "food orchestrator," in order to see what happens to the food and service during the busy dinner hours.

One might also code by **sentence or paragraph**. Here you might ask: What is the major idea brought out in this sentence or paragraph (of an interview, fieldnote, or document)? Give it a name. Then go back and do more detailed analysis on that concept. This approach to coding can be used at any time, but is especially useful when you have several categories already defined and now want to code around them.

A third way is to take **an entire document**, observation, or interview and ask: What seems to be going on here? What makes this document the same or different from the previous one that I coded? Having answered these questions, you might return to the data and specifically analyze for those similarities or differences.

Writing your Code Notes

Initial names for concepts are often written right on your interviews, fieldnotes, or other documents. Categories and the concepts pertaining to them are then taken from the pages and written as *code notes*, a type of memo. (These are discussed in Chapter 12.) There are many different specific ways of doing this recording, and each person must find the method that works best for himself or herself.

Coding is fun, isn't it? You never know what you might discover in a simple encounter. But the best is yet to come. So

move now to the next chapter where we will discuss techniques
you can use to increase your theoretical sensitivity during open
coding.

Summary

Concepts are the basic building blocks of theory. Open coding in grounded theory method is the analytic process by which
concepts are identified and developed in terms of their properties and dimensions. The basic analytic procedures by which
this is accomplished are: the asking of questions about data; and
the making of comparisons for similarities and differences between each incident, event, and other instances of phenomena.
Similiar events and incidents are labeled and grouped to form
categories.

6

Techniques for Enhancing
Theoretical Sensitivity

Up to now in our discussion on analysis we have remained strictly with the data in front of us (that which we observed in the restaurant). You could go on in this manner, *coding only what you see*. Notice what we've said, "only what you see." The trouble is that researchers often fail to see much of what is there because they come to analytic sessions wearing blinders, composed of assumptions, experience, and immersion in the literature. Oh, you are saying, "not me!" The problem is that you are not always aware how much these blinders color your interpretation of events until someone else points it out.

Let's take an example. Suppose you were driving by a park on a weekday morning about 9:30 a.m. and you see two dirty, shabbily dressed, unshaven men. They are sitting on a park bench drinking from what appears to be a wine bottle wrapped in a brown paper bag. What's your immediate reaction to this scenario? Two homeless winos drinking again. Perhaps! But maybe its about sharing, friendship, a form of interaction, survival, loneliness, and/or broken dreams. We'll never know until we look beneath the obvious.

Not that our assumptions, experience, and knowledge are necessarily bad, in and of themselves. Recall that earlier we said that these are helpful in developing theoretical sensitivity. It's just that we have to challenge our assumptions, delve beneath our experience, and look beyond the literature if we are to uncover phenomena and arrive at new theoretical formulations.

To discover theory in data we need theoretical sensitivity, the ability to "see" with analytic depth what is there. Later in the research project, theoretical sensitivity develops from working with the materials themselves. But in the early analytic stages, we need ways of opening up our thinking about the phenomena we are studying. The techniques we are about to present have been designed expressly to enable us to do this by using experience and knowledge to advantage, rather than to obscure vision. We cannot emphasize strongly enough the value of these techniques both for novices and experienced researchers. Since they are used all through the research process, in each of the types of coding, we discuss them at this point in the book.

What Techniques Are Designed To Do

(1) Steer your thinking out of the confines of both technical literature and personal experience.
(2) Help you to avoid standard ways of thinking about phenomena.
(3) Stimulate the inductive process.
(4) Focus on what is before you so that data can't be taken for granted.
(5) Allow for clarification or debunking of assumptions made by the people who appear in the data.
(6) Help you to listen to what people are saying and what they can possibly mean.

(7) Stop you from rushing past "diamonds in the rough" when examining the data.

(8) Force the asking of questions and the giving of provisional answers.

(9) Allow fruitful labeling, although provisionally.

(10) Allow exploration or clarification of the possible meanings of concepts.

(11) Discover properties and dimensions in data.

The Use of Questioning

The purpose behind the use of questioning is to open up the data: think of potential categories, their properties and dimensions. They help you to ask questions more precisely in the next interviews, or of any pertinent readings in the literature. We are not implying that these questions represent what is "really" in this data, rather we are referring to what future data collection and analysis could tell us, if we knew what questions to ask.

There are certain general questions that can be raised quite automatically about the data. Each question is likely to stimulate a series of more specific and related questions, which in turn lead to the development of categories, properties, and their dimensions. The basic questions are **Who? When? Where? What? How? How Much?** and **Why?**

Let's stop here and apply the questions to a situation so that you can see what we mean. Suppose you are investigating how arthritics handle their pain. You sit down with your interviews in front of you and read the quotation that appears below. But, keep in mind that the focus of your analysis is on how arthritics handle their pain. Naturally, in order to do so you must understand the meaning of that pain and even of the arthritis for them, since these play a large part in how people manage their condition. The questions that you ask will help you to get at all of this information. Here is the quoted passage from a woman's interview:

> Pain relief is a major problem when you have arthritis. Sometimes the pain is worse than other times, but when it gets really bad, whew! It hurts so bad, you don't want to get out of bed. You don't feel like doing anything. Any relief you get from drugs that you take is only temporary or partial.

The following is obvious from the data. It tells us that pain is a problem for her: **pain experience**. Also that her pain has the property of varying in **intensity** from bad to not so bad. Under conditions when the pain is bad, there are two consequences: her activity is limited, **activity limitation**; and she stays in bed, **bed bound**. The data also informs us that she used drugs to relieve her pain: **pain relief**, another category. **Self-administration of drugs** is a strategy for obtaining relief from pain. **Pain relief** has two properties: **duration** (it is temporary) and **degree** (it is partial).

Let's see what we have here. We have two categories: **Pain Experience** and **Pain Relief**. These two categories emerged from our initial coding. They are categories because, as you can see, other concepts (subcategories) can be subsumed under them as properties, conditions, consequences, and strategies. That's not bad, for a few minutes of analysis.

We could go on in this manner, coding each interview. Hopefully, we would further develop these categories and new ones would also emerge. But this could be a long tedious process, and how much we got out of the data would depend very much on our theoretical sensitivity. So, now let's see how we might increase our sensitivity by applying our list of questions to our chosen area of study. We will apply the questions not necessarily to this particular woman with arthritis but **in general to people** who have arthritis. Notice that in order to ask the subquestions under each major heading you must draw upon personality experience, and professional experience, if you have any, as well as from the technical literature. But, we are using all of these sources in a free associative, creative manner.

Who provides pain relief to people with arthritis? Is it always provided by themselves or might someone else provide it? For instance, do they ever go to a doctor's office, a clinic, an emergency room to get relief? Do persons other than physicians provide a source of relief, such as physical therapists who use water techniques, or show them how to position or move their bodies or ways of moving that produce less strain on painful sites? What about technicians who might teach them bio-feedback techniques for reducing pain? Or spiritual advisors who might teach meditation for the same purpose?

What gives relief? Here it is drugs, but what else might people in pain do? Try different positions? Meditation? Keeping still? Heat? Quiet activities like reading or watching TV that might take their minds away from the pain? What are the latest forms of therapy talked about in the technical literature? Are there any special clinics or places, whose purpose is solely to teach people how to handle their pain?

How is the pain experienced and handled? How much relief is needed? Do all persons experience pain in the same way? If not, how does it vary? What does this arthritic person mean when she says the pain is intense? Is it more intense when she is tired or not tired, distracted or not distracted, depressed or not depressed? Does she handle the pain by complaining, not complaining; moving, not moving; obtaining relief by herself, seeking help elsewhere? How do other people handle their pain? Is a lot of relief needed or a little?

When does the pain occur and when does she institute relief? Is the pain worse in the morning or at night? More intense after movement or during? Does she take medication before moving, at the first signs of pain, or does she wait until it becomes intense? Does she try other methods of relief before taking her medication?

Why is pain relief important? What happens when the pain is not relieved? What happens when it is? How does this affect her activity level? Her outlook on life? How she feels about the arthritis itself and its future course?

There are also a set of *temporal* questions that can be asked here: **frequency, duration, rate, timing**. Let's see what happens when we apply these to our anecdotal note.

Frequency? How often must the pain be relieved? Each hour, each day? Is the pain and the relief that follows predictable?

Duration? How long does the pain last? How long does the relief last? Are there certain things that can be done in conjunction with pain relief measures that prolong or shorten their effect?

Rate? How quickly or slowly is relief obtained? How quickly or slowly does it vanish: suddenly, gradually?

Timing? Are pain relief medications given at specific times of the day? How much time must elapse before the next dose can be given? If it involves exercises, how long does this take?

One could also ask *spatial* types of questions: How much space does special equipment take? Is storage a problem? Or *technological* types of questions, such as: What kinds of special equipment are needed? Is special skill required to use it? What are its size, cost, movability (drugs are movable)?

You can see now that you have a lot more to think about than when you first started thinking about the data on pain. All the answers to the questions raised may not be in the actual data that are before you, but there is no need for concern on that account. It is up to you to take the questions to the next interviews and analytic sessions to look for the answers. Not that you necessarily will go down the list asking all those questions. Many of the answers will come up in the next interviews without your even asking the questions, only this time you will, in a manner of speaking, "hear them." You will be looking at your data in terms of them, picking up cues, asking for more detail. Also, you will be far more sensitive when examining data during the next analytic sessions, and asking those kinds of questions of the data. If no answers are found, then it's necessary to ask: "To whom might I speak to next to find these answers?" (Don't forget what you learned earlier, that your answers will be conceptualized and grouped into categories, their properties and dimensions, just as above.)

Analysis of a Word, Phrase, Sentence

Next, we will show you that one does not necessarily need a whole paragraph or a list of questions in order to "open up" the data. This can be done with a sentence, a phrase, or sometimes even with a single word.

Analysis of a word, phrase, or sentence is an especially valuable exercise because it can teach you how to raise questions about possible meanings, whether assumed or intended, by a speaker and those around him or her. It can also help to bring out your own assumptions about what is being said, and force you to be examine and question them. This exercise can be invaluable as an opening gambit even for experienced analysts, because even they bring preconceptions and perspectives to their analytic sessions.

Usually, when anyone sees words he or she will assign meanings to them, derived from common usage or experience. We often believe that because we would act and feel in a particular manner, that this, of course, is what the respondent means by those words. That belief is not necessarily accurate. Take a word—any word—and ask people what it means to them. The word "red" is a good example. One person may say: "bulls, lipstick, and blood." Another might respond: "passion." Perhaps for you it means a favorite dress, a rose, a glamorous sports car, or none of the above. As an exercise, we suggest that you list all of the thoughts that come to mind when you think about the word "red." Amazing isn't it! Red is far more than a color. It has sentiment, feeling, texture, sensation, smell, and action all built into it. These associations are derived from the meanings we have come to associate with this word over the years, whether for personal or cultural reasons.

The **procedure** here is to first scan a document, or at least a couple of pages of it, then return to any word, phrase, or sentence that struck you as significant, important, or of interest. The item should be one that you wish to think about more deeply. Then list all of its possible meanings, from the most probable to the most improbable.

To show you how you might use this technique, we will illustrate how it was used in a research seminar to open up the analysis of one student's data.

The place is a classroom. The student's research interest is in disability. She wants help in analyzing an interview done with a young disabled man. The word from his interview that the seminar chose to work on was *once*. It was taken from the phrase, "Once I'm in the shower."

I = Instructor
S = Student (any student)

I. Knowing the context of the interviewee's action, what might *once* mean?

S. The man felt **independent** once he was in the shower. A *consequence*.

I. Where else might he feel independent, once he was there?

S. In bed and in the wheelchair.

I. Where might he feel **dependent** once he was there? Another *consequence*, but related to a variation in activity.

S. When faced with a flight of stairs.

I. What else could once mean?

S. A *condition* for what might come next in the interviewee's activity.

S. The end of one action and the beginning of the next. The idea of **phasing** or **sequence** of action.

I. Let's take another situation where the word once might be said and compare it to this one. Perhaps by making this comparison it will generate other potential meanings of the word. The situation is a track race. The speaker says: "Once the gun went off, I forgot about all the months of grueling training."

S. Rates of movement through each phase of action. *Property* of time and idea of *Process*.

S. Preparation that goes before the "once." *Condition* of training or preparation that is involved before activity can occur.

S. The interviewee's effort in getting to the once. *Property* of effort and *consequence* of achievement.

The class went on for an hour discussing the word "once," exploring possible meanings, raising questions, and naming phenomena, none of which were imposed on this data. That is, no one implied that any of the possible meanings evolving from this session necessarily applied to this particular disabled man or this one instance of activity. What the exercise did was to give the presenting student a possible range of meanings that could be associated with the word "once," thus sensitizing her to what she might find analytically in this and other interviews.

Again, note how one word can imply any number of meanings. Notice also that we did not stray far from the situation under study and kept our analysis of "once" related to activity. But even in this instance, thinking about a single word gave rise to considerations of process, conditions, consequences, variations, and so forth, which can be applied to the student's future thinking about activity and the disabled.

To avoid repetition, we will not give examples of the application of this technique to phrases or sentences. Suffice to say, one could obtain a great deal of analytic mileage by using this same procedure with them also. There is so much potential in a sentence such as: "The first series of cancer treatments didn't work." One might begin by asking what possible meanings might be associated with each word separately, then together: cancer, treatment, then cancer treatment, and the phrase "first series." Since we are focused now on these words (and possible categories derived from our analysis) we will be more likely to ask our respondents, if they fail to tell us, exactly what meanings these words have for them. This is in contrast to a common glossing over of their meanings in interviews, which is often done because the meanings are readily assumed when a person speaks. **Unless we validate possible meanings** during interaction with the speakers, or train ourselves to ask what meanings the various analytically salient terms have for our respondents, we limit the potential development of our theory.

Further Analysis Through Comparisons

In the chapter on open coding we noted that the making of comparisons was essential to identifying and categorizing concepts. We shall now discuss the use of comparisons further, but this time as a stimulus to theoretical sensitivity.

The purpose of the comparisons we speak of here is similar to other techniques we have discussed. They are to help you break through assumptions and also to uncover specific dimensions. Note, however, that in order to make these comparisons you must draw upon personal knowledge, professional knowledge, and the technical literature.

The Flip-Flop Technique

Suppose you are studying the computer industry. You read the first few pages of your fieldnotes and notice that IBM is a giant in the industry. In fact, it dominates this industry. Now, you might wonder what does domination mean in terms of the industry as a whole, what are its consequences for competitors' pricing and sales tactics, for their defensive maneuvers and the organization of their production? But the answers to these questions do not appear to be in your current data. Staring at the data, your mind goes blank. Nothing seems to strike you.

When this happens, you might break through your mental paralysis by using the flip-flop technique. That is, by turning the concept of domination upside down, and imagining the very opposite: An industry not dominated by any one company but where company influence or power is widely distributed throughout the industry (as in the clothing or building industries). What you are doing here is making a comparison at the *extremes of one dimension* of this industry: *highly* to *not at all*.

Now, when you return to your fieldwork or to look at published materials, you will be more focused and more likely to notice properties and dimensions that you might have overlooked had you not done this little exercise. **The exercise should also help you to think analytically rather than descriptively about data, to generate provisional categories and their properties, and to think about generative questions.**

Below we will show this technique in action, using another example. This time our area of interest is the **Body.** We have decided to learn about the body by studying the world of weight lifting. We chose this particular option because we have had some experience with weight lifting, and have easy access to observational sites and potential interviewees, since it can sometimes be difficult to gain access and obtain subjects in unfamiliar areas. We must be aware, however, that our familiarity with the area of study might hinder our analysis by keeping us too focused on the observable reality as such.

To begin with, we spend a few hours observing one evening at a gym and keeping notes on what was observed. Later that evening, while doing the analysis, we come up with the following categories: body strength, body shaping, body monitoring, body training, and body movement. These are all subcategories of still a larger category, which at this point we call "Building Up the Body." Now we decide to take one of our subcategories, **body strength,** and open it up in order to uncover potential properties and dimensions that might apply to it. We examine our data but nothing very interesting is forthcoming. We're stuck. So, we decide to think about a sport in which body strength is not essential or only minimal, like trout fishing. We will do a comparison of trout fishing with weight lifting.

Now, what strikes us about trout fishing? Well, practically anyone of any age can fish for trout, from a four-year-old to an eighty-five-year-old. **Age** then might be an important point to consider when looking at weight lifters in relation to strength. What else strikes us about trout fishing? It is done outdoors, **Place.** This presents another factor to examine. It may be relevant to weight lifting in general but not necessarily to strength.

Let's go on. You usually don't catch trout with your hands, you need **special equipment**. This you need for weight lifting also. But now we need to ask, what is the relationship of strength to equipment? Is the latter used to build strength? How? The greater the strength the more weight (via equipment) you can lift. Trout fishing is not usually **dangerous**, unless you fall in the water and can't swim. Can having too much or too little strength be dangerous when using equipment? In what ways? What happens if you think you have more strength than you actually have? Trout fishing is usually done in the early morning or day **time**. What about weight lifting? Are there different times in a day, week, month when a person's body strength peaks or wears down, and for what reason?

Instead of making comparisons with a completely different sport, we could also do the following kind of flip-flop. We could compare a 250 pound male weight lifter with a 100 pound female one. Let's see what we get out of this comparison. The male has more **strength** than the female, as evidenced by the amount of weight he lifts. Hmmm, where does his strength come from? He has more muscle, body mass. True, but why? Some strength comes from differences in **internal body regulators**, hormonal differences between men and women. Can men then take extra hormones as a condition for enhancing their strength? Can women? Since these are male hormones, what might be the *consequences* to women taking steroids, in addition to extra strength? What are the consequences for men? Is it **legal** to take steroids? If not, why not? How do they then obtain them?

Besides taking hormones, how else might women enhance their strength? By initially having 250 pound men **help** them, while lifting heavy weights. With time and practice, they can then gradually develop the ability to lift heavier weights by themselves, unless this is much beyond their **body capacity**. Do men sometimes enlist the help of other men or women? If so, then this tells us that weight lifting sometimes has an *interactional component*. Always, sometimes, when? What other *strategies* might men and women use to enhance their strength—concentration, getting psyched up, urging by others?

Even from this brief analysis, you can see how by taking the subcategory of **body strength**, and using the flip-flop technique to think comparatively, we have opened up our analysis. We have raised questions to pursue in further observations and interviews. We have also developed potential subcategories of body strength and their associated dimensions, which in turn lead to strategies that might be used to increase body strength. We have also related some potential consequences to the use of those strategies. With this in mind, we can now return to our fieldnotes and observations with more sensitivity to the topic than previously. Then we can go back into the field again to test our hypotheses. To open up the other categories (body shaping, body training, body monitoring, and so forth) we could use this or other techniques already discussed.

Systematic Comparison of Two or More Phenomena

Let us now consider a different problem. Assume that we have come to our analysis of **body** already steeped in the technical literature. In fact, we have been very impressed with a couple of the studies on "body image." Without even being aware, we have allowed these studies to color the approach that we have taken to our analysis of the data. Though not obvious to us, the bias may be noticed by colleagues or thesis committee members. If they mention it, we are astounded and confused. Take another situation. We are so accustomed to looking at problems in certain ways, that when this way fails to uncover the reasons for problems we see, we go around and around in our old ways of thinking and can't seem to break through.

What can we do to break out from our patterns of thinking, while still retaining what is important from our readings or experience? **The use of systematic comparisons early in our analysis is one way.** Here's how it works.

Take what you know about body image from the literature and your own experience and start coding this phenomenon very systematically, just as you have been taught up to this point. You should have some concepts, categories, and properties.

Now take one of those categories, say, weight. The research literature tells you that being either over weight or under weight is one of the conditions that negatively affects body image. We can begin by making what we call a *close-in comparison*, say comparing an overweight woman with another who is of normal weight and also physically attractive. We would want to ask questions that systematically bring out similarities and differences between our two women. For example: What happens when a physically attractive woman walks down the street, especially if she is wearing a tight fitting dress? People might turn to look appreciatively. All people? Well, some men and maybe some women. How else might they look at her? Some men might look at her lecherously, or at least with appreciation. Some women might look at her with admiration or with disgust.

Are these sentiments conveyed to this woman as she is walking down the street? That is, how would she know what others are thinking or feeling? How might it affect her body image to realize that a man was looking at her admiringly? Lecherously? Does it mean as much to her to be admired by a woman as by a man? (These questions help you to begin to think about "under what conditions" body image develops, and also to think about the interactional component involved in its development.)

Now you might ask yourself: How do people look at an overweight woman walking down the street in a tight dress? Do they look at her appreciatively or with disgust? Under what conditions might they look at her admiringly? With what strategies might they convey their feelings? What consequences might each of these have for her body image? Would she be more likely or less likely to wear a tight dress, if she were aware of what they were thinking? Might her wearing such a tight dress indicate that she didn't care what people think about her, that, in fact, she is satisfied with her body? Why might this woman feel this way, while other overweight people do not? These questions get you to thinking that perhaps not all overweight women have a poor body image. With this insight you can go back to the field and interview women to find out why. Then you might systematically compare the responses against those of women with a poor body image against those with a good one.

If we needed to approach one of the women to ask for directions, which would you feel most comfortable asking? Why? What messages would your comfort or discomfort convey? What part(s) of the body might the person who is asking directions focus on, while asking about the directions? Try various possibilities and list potential consequences that these might have for body image. Also, how might you feel if the physically attractive woman brushes your question off as a come-on, while the overweight woman takes great pains to explain the directions to you? How might this then be conveyed back to the women? These questions open you up to consider all sorts of possible consequences of being overweight, with some of those consequences not necessarily being negative. These consequences feed back, of course, into the considerations you take into account as you develop this category of body image.

Now let's use our creativity to conjure up a situation involving these two women that might be quite the opposite from what we would expect, and ask some questions about this situation. The scene is a dating game TV show. A man behind a screen, after listening to two potential dates respond to his questions, thinks he would like to date the one named Annie. He passes up on Joan. The audience chuckles, and boos his choice. When he meets Joan, he sees what the audience is reacting to. Joan is physically attractive. Wowie! But he recalls that her responses to the questions were dull and she didn't seem like she'd be much fun. Annie on the other hand turns out to be overweight. Our man, after the initial shock, turns out to be quite delighted with his choice. Annie seems very comfortable with herself, has a great personality, and loves to dance. She certainly didn't fit the image of our stereotype of the woman who has a poor body image.

Now we have to stop and ask why? Where do our stereotypes come from? Is it our image or their image that we are placing on these women? And might an attractive woman have a poor body image? Why? Does it all have to do with body size? How is body image conveyed to others? Asking such questions and then following through in collecting and analyzing data soon moves you away from the technical literature on body image, opening up other possibilities to follow up on. While in the end you may come to the same conclusions as those in the literature, **your theoretical explanations will be far more dense because your questions took you away from the standard ways of thinking, and allowed exploration of other avenues of thought and hopefully gave new insights into the problem.**

Far-Out Comparisons

Before closing this section, we will briefly mention the use of *far-out comparisons*. Analysts usually stay as close to their substantive areas as possible when making comparisons, fearing that they can't possibly learn anything that can be applied to their area by making a far-out comparison. That assumption is *not* true. Let's return to our study of the weight lifters. This time we want to think about equipment and body building. To come up with some questions and categories about the relationship between the two, we decide to make a comparison between weight lifting and playing the violin. Now, what can the latter teach us about equipment and body building? Let's find out.

Violinists need equipment. Body builders need equipment. Violinists can carry their equipment with them. Some body building equipment can be carried, some is too heavy to carry about, property of **portability**. What did the gyms themselves: Are they all stationary or are there portable gyms? Who uses such gyms? Violins have strings that can break? Body building equipment can also break down, property of **breakability**?

What happens on a busy night and some of the equipment is broken? Would you continue to work out at a gym in which there is always broken equipment? There are industries that build and repair violins. There must also be industries that build and repair weight lifting equipment. Now we are getting at some of the macroscopic conditions, the **industries** that provide and service equipment. What are these? What about the relevant state of technology, and so forth? The equipment that a violinist uses usually belongs to him or her. The weight lifter may own his or her own equipment, but might also use someone else's equipment. This not only brings out the property of **ownership** but brings us to ask further questions such as: Who owns the equipment? What does that mean in terms of where weight training takes place? What kinds of weight lifting equipment might one own? Under what conditions might one use it at home? Under what conditions might one go to a gym to use theirs? Violinists usually have teachers. Do weight lifters have teachers who demonstrate how to use equipment? They have **body trainers**. Who are these trainers? What qualifications do they have? Under what conditions might one use a trainer? Under what conditions might one not use a trainer? Does everyone need a trainer to learn how to lift weights? What other roles besides showing one how to use equipment do trainers play?

As you can see, the possibilities that are opened up through the use of comparisons are endless. Yet we need not go on making comparisons for hours, but should do so just until we are freed of whatever is blocking us or we have a list of properties and dimensions to pursue. Then we can go back to our data, but this time ready to make new discoveries because we have a little more insight about what is "really on the page," or should be there.

Waving the Red Flag

There is one more technique that we would like to pass on to you before concluding our chapter. It is called waving the red flag. Again, this technique has to do with helping the analyst to see beyond the obvious in data. Assumptions that are based on cultural perspectives are especially difficult to recognize because everyone of the same cultural heritage, for the most part, thinks the same way so that no one is likely to question you for making these shared assumptions.

For example, one of our students was studying the use of Asian interpreters in clinics. When recounting an incident, the student explained that sometimes male interpreters are called upon to interpret for female clients. The use of men in these cases is problematic because some issues, like sex and female gynecological problems, are considered very sensitive areas and never discussed in mixed gender company. The instructor asked, "Are these areas never discussed?" The student replied, "Never." The instructor began to vary the conditions. "Under conditions when a woman's life is threatened would these issues be brought up?" "Oh, no!" the student replied, "they are taboo." Now the instructor, drawing upon experience, knew that all cultures have sensitive areas but they also have ways of handling these, and that under certain conditions one might disregard these taboos or find ways around them. The student really knew this too, but she was so immersed in the data before her that she didn't think to question this matter. Had the student continued to accept the obvious rather than to question it, she would have missed the whole issue of how sensitive situations are handled in various Asian cultures using interpreters, certainly an important part of her analysis.

To emphasize our essential point: You should become very sensitive to certain words and phrases. Ones such as: "Never," "Always," "It couldn't possibly be that way," "Everyone knows that's the way it is done," "There is no need for discussion." Every time you hear such words or phrases, you should wave a red flag—an imaginary flag, of course.

These words and phrases should be taken as signals to take a closer look. What is going on here? What do you mean *never*? Or always? Why is this so? Never, under what conditions?

How is this state of never maintained? What are its consequences? What happens if never is not maintained. That is, if some poor ignorant person never does whatever he or she is not supposed to do? Are there certain strategies to get around that never? How are unquestioning or accepting people culturally trained to believe in never? Do people act in that manner but not believe it? Believe it but not act on it?

The analytic issue here is never to take anything for granted. The minute that you do, you foreclose on many possibilities that may be the key to uncovering the answer to one of your research problems.

Issues and Concerns

Over the years we have noticed that students sometimes have concerns about using these techniques. It is important to discuss the concerns, for they may be yours too.

(1) Students are often awed when they see these techniques at work in class. They think that the instructor has some sort of magical ability that they could never duplicate. Like a magician, he or she can turn straw (the data) into gold (theory).

(2) Students often become so engrossed in the data before them—data are so fascinating—that they can't free themselves. They seem to forget that they have ever learned the techniques, then later wonder why they can't see anything in the data but the same old stuff. They may finally come to us, saying "Help me to get out of this analytic rut."

(3) Sometimes students are afraid to use the techniques systematically because they think that they will then somehow impose something on the data that is not there. They fear that they can't really learn anything about their substantive area of study by straying too far away from the data.

(4) Students are often unsure of how and when to use the techniques. They are concerned that they have to use them during every interview and with each analytic session.

Let us respond to these concerns. First, believe us, the ability to use these techniques doesn't constitute any kind of magic. You too can turn a little data into effective theoretical ideas after learning to use these techniques. All it takes is patience, much practice, and trust in your capacities to learn. Second, the techniques have to be used, if you want to "open up" the data and set free whatever degree of creative ability and theoretical sensitivity that you have. If you don't use these, your discoveries will be minimal and your theories conceptually thin and poorly validated.

Third, never impose anything on the data. This means that initially any concepts, categories, or hypotheses that come out of the use of these creative procedures are to be considered provisional. They function to sensitize a researcher to know what to look for. They are designed to free up thinking and awaken sensitivity. The ideas that evolve from the use of these techniques should never be confused with data; they are only hypothetical possibilities that must always be supported by actual data.

Fourth, the techniques are to be used only as aids to analysis, *not* done with every fieldnote or interview. They are especially useful in analyzing the first few interviews, field observations and documents, because they help to "see" what is in the data. Even here they are not to be used in connection with every word, phrase, or paragraph. Later in the analysis, the techniques are also very useful when you become puzzled, feel blocked, or are unsure of where to go next in your analysis or data collection. **They are effective tools. Like all tools, however, you will have to learn how and when to use them. But use them!** Experiment with them and discover your own ways of getting them to function effectively for your particular purposes. Bear in mind also that while we are introducing these procedures in connection with open coding, their **usage is just**

as important when you reach an analytic standstill in axial and even selective coding.

While your intention is to do serious analytic work with these techniques, and although learning to use them skillfully and easily may be hard work, there is no reason why this can't be fun. It might seem facetious to say "relax and enjoy yourself," but at least don't confuse the seriousness of the work with the enjoyment you can gain from it.

Summary

Each of us brings to the analysis of data our biases, assumptions, patterns of thinking, and knowledge gained from experience and reading. These can block our seeing what is significant in the data, or prevent us from moving from descriptive to theoretical levels of analysis. There are certain techniques that can be used to prevent or rectify these problems. They include: the use of questioning; analysis of a single word, phrase, or sentence; the flip-flop procedure; the making of comparisons, both close-in and far-out; and waving the red flag. All it takes is practice, the more the better, and creative imagination.

In fact, such creative imagination as you possess is very likely to be improved by assiduous practice of these techniques. In the beginning you can also practice on someone else's data, or on any document—even a magazine article— since you may find this is psychologically easier than always facing your own data. But remember, practice of these techniques is a necessity until you find their use has become more or less automatic for you.

Also, it may help your learning these techniques if near the end of an analytic session you review the actual steps taken during the session in analyzing your data. This enhances your awareness of how you have used the procedures and with what results. Paradoxically, an occasional review like this leads eventually to using them less self-consciously, more naturally.

Axial Coding

Definition of Terms

Axial Coding: A set of procedures whereby data are put back together in new ways after open coding, by making connections between categories. This is done by utilizing a coding paradigm involving conditions, context, action/interactional strategies and consequences.

Causal Conditions: Events, incidents, happenings that lead to the occurrence or development of a phenomenon.

Phenomenon: The central idea, event, happening, incident about which a set of actions or interactions are directed at managing, handling, or to which the set of actions is related.

Context: The specific set of properties that pertain to a phenomenon; that is, the locations of events or incidents pertaining to a phenomenon along a dimensional range. Context represents the particular set of conditions within which the action/interactional strategies are taken.

Intervening Conditions: The structural conditions bearing on action/interactional strategies that pertain to a phenomenon. They facilitate or constrain the strategies taken within a specific context.

Action/Interaction: Strategies devised to manage, handle, carry out, respond to a phenomenon under a specific set of perceived conditions.

Consequences: Outcomes or results of action and interaction.

Open coding (as in Chapter 5) fractures the data and allows one to identify some categories, their properties, and dimensional locations. Axial coding puts those data back together in new ways by *making connections between a category and its subcategories.* Here, we are not talking about the relating of several main categories to form an overall theoretical formulations (see Chapter 8), but the development of what will eventually become one of several main categories. In other words, we are still concerned with the development of a category, but development beyond properties and dimensions.

In axial coding our focus is on specifying a category (*phenomenon*) in terms of the conditions that give rise to it; the *context* (its specific set of properties) in which it is embedded; the action/interactional *strategies* by which it is handled, managed, carried out; and the *consequences* of those strategies. These specifying features of a category give it precision, thus we refer to them as *subcategories.* In essence, they too are categories, but because we relate them to a category in some form of relationships, we add the prefix "sub."

You recall in the chapter on Techniques for Enhancing Theoretical Sensitivity (Chapter 6) that in some of our examples of analyses we used terms such as "conditions," "strategies," "consequences." As we coded, these terms came up, showing us that as soon as we break data apart in open coding, we just naturally start to put them back together in a relational form.

**Though open and axial coding are distinct analytic proce-
dures, when the researcher is actually engaged in analysis he
or she alternates between the two modes.**

Before we enter into a discussion of how category specification takes place through axial coding, we would like you to
consider the following points.

(1) During open coding many different categories are identified. Some of these will pertain to specific phenomena such as
pain, pain management, body strength, body image. Other categories will refer to conditions that relate to those phenomena.
Still other categories will denote action/interactional strategies
used to manage, handle, respond to that phenomenon. Finally,
some categories will refer to consequences of action/interac-
tion, again in relationship to a specific phenomenon.

(2) The actual conceptual labels placed on categories won't
necessarily point to whether a category denotes a condition,
strategy, or consequence. You have to identify them as such. For
example, the concept of **pain relief** does not include the term
consequence anywhere in its name. Yet, in some instances (depending upon the focus of the study), pain relief may be a consequence of action taken to relieve pain. Nor are conditions,
strategies, or consequences necessarily spelled out as such in
the interviews or documents we are analyzing, though an incident or event may implicitly suggest these. Consider the
following phrase: "When I have (condition) arthritic pain (phenomenon), I take aspirin (strategy). After a while, I feel better
(consequence)." Notice how we have spelled out the paradigm
features.

(3) Every category, whether a phenomenon indicating category, or one of its specifying subcategories, will have properties. These can be dimensionalized, giving the category further
specification. For example, the subcategory pain relief (consequence) has general properties such as duration, degree, potential for causing side effects, and so forth, which will be specific

for each case. While the phenomenon of arthritic pain has general properties like degree, duration, and intensity, again these are specific for each case. In coding a document about pain (or any other phenomenon), each event or incident can be given a specific dimensional location in terms of these properties. This dimensional location has relevance for theory integration (see Chapter 8 on Selective Coding).

(4) In axial coding subcategories are related to their categories through what we call the *paradigm model*. This model and how it is used to relate subcategories to a category in axial coding will be explained as you read further.

The Paradigm Model

In grounded theory **we link subcategories to a category in a set of relationships** denoting casual conditions, phenomenon, context, intervening conditions, action/interactional strategies, and consequences. Highly simplified, the model looks something like this:

(A) CAUSAL CONDITIONS → (B) PHENOMENON →
(C) CONTEXT → (D) INTERVENING CONDITIONS →
(E) ACTION/INTERACTION STRATEGIES →
(F) CONSEQUENCES.

Use of this model will enable you to think systematically about data and to relate them in very complex ways. Just as now when you encounter certain life situations you automatically rely on a causal model (something has happened because of this cause or condition) to explain to yourself and to others why it may have occurred. With continued practice you can easily learn to think in terms of the more complicated paradigm model. Unless you make use of this model, your grounded theory analyses will lack density and precision.

Before moving on to the mechanics of how categories are related by means of the paradigm, each of its features will be explained more thoroughly.

Phenomenon

This is the central idea, event, happening, about which a set of actions/interactions is directed at **managing or handling, or to which the set is related**. We identify the *phenomenon* by asking questions such as: What is this data referring to? What is the action/interaction all about? (See Chapter 5 for details.)

Causal Conditions

This term refers to the events or incidents that lead to the occurrence or development of a phenomenon. For example, if interested in the phenomenon of pain, we might discover that breaking a leg or having arthritis can lead to pain. Such incidents cause or bring about the pain experience. Using the paradigm model, a pain event might be diagramed like this:

Causal condition	$\rightarrow$	Phenomenon
Breaking a leg or having arthritis		pain

In reality, a single *causal condition* rarely produces a phenomenon. Remember we are looking at pain associated with a broken leg. It is the properties of this broken leg (and person to whom it belongs) that combine together to lead to that pain. Now we have to be specific about describing the break; that is, to identify its properties and dimensional location along those properties. We might say that there was more than one break— two (number of fractures), and that one of the breaks is a compound rather than simple break (type of break); furthermore the person who suffered the break is neither unconscious nor a paraplegic, so that the nervous system is intact and functioning (degree of sensation). We could take pain and also look at its specific properties and dimensions, which in fact should be explainable by looking back at the specific dimensions of the causal conditions. For example, one might expect with multiple fractures, a compound break, and high sensation being present in the leg, that the **intensity** of the pain would be high. As to **duration** of the pain, we might say that it is continuous. Now our diagram looks something like this:

Causal Condition	→	*Phenomenon*
A broken leg		Pain

Properties of Broken Leg	*Specific Dimensions of Pain*	
Multiple fractures	intensity	high
Compound break	duration	continuous
Sensation present	location	lower leg

You might be thinking that breaking a leg or having arthritis are phenomena in and of themselves. That's quite true. But remember our focus is on pain, not on arthritis or the break. Our interest in either is only as a condition for that pain, and in being able to explain the amount, type, duration, and so forth, of the pain by looking back at the specific properties of the causal condition. It is important to point out here that a causal condition can be any event (such as a certain behavior, something that is said, something that someone does), as well as a chance event. It all depends upon the situation.

Causal conditions, or antecedent conditions as they are sometimes called, are often pointed to in the data by terms such as: "when," "while," "since," "because," "due to," "on account of." Even when such cues are missing, you can often locate causal conditions by focusing on a phenomenon, and systematically looking back through your data for those events, happenings, or incidents that seem to precede it.

Context

A *context* **represents the specific set of properties that pertain to a phenomenon;** that is, the location of events or incidents pertaining to a phenomenon along a dimensional range. (See Chapter 5 for a review, if you are unclear about this.) Context, at the same time, **is also the particular set of conditions within which the action/interaction strategies are taken to manage, handle, carry out, and respond to a specific phenomenon.** It is context that we are describing when we say

"Under conditions of intense pain of long duration, we take such and such a measure to control it."

To clarify this point, let's return to our example of the broken leg. A broken leg leads to pain. Knowing only this, as we've said, makes it difficult to treat. We have to know the specifics about the cause, as well as the pain to be able to treat it. About the broken leg, we would want to know specifically **when** it was broken, **how**, the **number** of fractures, the **types** of fractures, whether **sensation** is present or absent from in the leg, and so forth. About the pain, we would want to know something about its **trajectory**, or course over time; also, its **duration**, its specific **location**, its **intensity**, and so forth.

Now we can say: Under the specific conditions of (a) being early in the pain trajectory; (b) having intense pain; (c) of relatively short duration; (d) that is located along the long bone of the lower leg, then we will take these measures to mitigate the pain.

Our diagram on pain, now, looks something like this:

Causal Condition	→	*Phenomenon*
A broken leg		Pain

Properties of Broken Leg	*Specific Dimensions of Pain*	
Multiple fractures	intensity	high
Compound break	duration	continuous
Sensation present	location	lower leg
Broken two hours ago	trajectory	early
Fall on icy street	obtained help	soon

Pain Management Context
Under Conditions Where Pain is:
continuous, of high intensity, located in lower leg, early in the trajectory, and where help was obtained soon, then:

Intervening Conditions

We now move to another set of conditions that relate to our phenomenon (category) under study. First we spoke of causal conditions, next we mentioned context, which is both the specific properties of a phenomenon and at the same time a set of conditions influencing action/interaction. Now we speak of *intervening conditions*. What are these? You might think of them as *the broader structural context* pertaining to a phenomenon. These conditions act to either facilitate or constrain the action/interactional strategies taken within a specific context. These too must be managed. An example of an intervening condition can be seen in the following statement. You are ill and need a given medical technology as treatment, but it can only be obtained at a distant medical center. Somehow in order to obtain that treatment, you will have to travel. In other words, you can't immediately act to receive the treatment, you have the distance to contend with.

Intervening conditions are the broad and general conditions bearing upon action/interactional strategies. These conditions include: time, space, culture, economic status, technological status, career, history, and individual biography. (More will be said about these, as well as how to weave these into analysis, in Chapter 10.) They range from those most distant to the situation, to those closer in. Let's return to our example of the broken leg to see how these particular conditions work to either facilitate or constrain action/interaction.

Suppose, a person's leg was broken while he or she was out in the woods rather than in the city and the person was alone rather than with someone. These conditions could make a difference in the amount of time that elapses before someone receives medical care and pain relief. Also important are biographical features such as age of the person, other illnesses or conditions present, past history with pain, and ideologies and philosophies about pain and its treatment, both those of the individual and those treating the pain. Then too, there are technological features such as procedures and medications available to manage the pain, knowledge about their usage, equipment available, and so forth.

We could continue to list intervening conditions, but the above is sufficient to clarify the point. Not all conditions will apply to every situation. It is up to you the analyst to identify which to apply and to weave them into the analysis, by showing how they facilitate or constrain action/interaction and when appropriate how action/interaction are managed.

Action/Interactional Strategies

Grounded theory is an *action/interactional oriented method of theory building*. Whether one is studying individuals, groups, or collectives, there is action/interaction, which is directed at managing, handling, carrying out, responding to a phenomenon as it exists in context or under a specific set of perceived conditions. The interactional component refers to self as well as other interaction.

Action/interaction has certain properties. First, it is **processual**, evolving in nature. Thus it can be studied in terms of sequences, or in terms of movement, or change over time. (See Chapter 9.) Second, the action/interaction about which we speak is **purposeful, goal oriented**, done for some reason—in response to or to manage a phenomenon. Therefore, it occurs through *strategies* and tactics. Though not all action/interaction is purposeful, it may be reflexive in some cases. Also, action/interaction may be taken for purposes unrelated to the phenomenon under question, but have consequences for that phenomenon. Say you are studying self-esteem in children. A child spills a glass of milk on the floor. The mother, tired from just having scrubbed the floor, yells at the child for spilling the milk. The child's self-esteem suffers because several of his friends are present, but that was not the mother's intent. Third, **failed action/interaction** is just as important to look for, as when action/interaction is actually taken or occurs. In other words, if someone should, or ordinarily would do something in a situation and he or she doesn't, then we must ask why? Fourth, as we mentioned earlier, there are always *intervening conditions* that either facilitate or constrain action/interaction. These conditions must be discovered too.

Once more returning to our diagram about pain, at this point it might look like this:

Causal Condition	→	*Phenomenon*
A broken leg		Pain

Properties of Broken Leg	*Specific Dimensions of Pain*	
Multiple fractures	intensity	high
Compound break	duration	continuous
Sensation present	location	lower leg
Broken two hours ago	trajectory	early
Fall in the woods	obtained help	long wait
	potential for	
	consequences	high

Pain Management Context
Under Conditions Where Pain is:
intense, continuous, located in the lower leg, early in the trajectory, there is a long wait for help and the potential for consequences is high, then:

Strategies for Pain Management
Splint the leg
Go for emergency help
Keep person warm

Intervening Conditions
Lack of training in first aid
No blanket
A long way to go for help

As with conditions, there are certain cues in your data that
point to strategies. They are action oriented verbs or participles.
They tell you that someone is doing or saying something in
response to a phenomenon. For example, if one were to study
work flow in a hospital unit and the role of the head nurse in
keeping the work flow going, we might see the following in our
data:

> When there are severe conflicts between the staff on the night shift
> and the conflicts begin to interfere with the work performance,
> then I come in at night and work with that shift for a while in order
> to assess what is going on.

Here we have a phenomenon (work flow) that is being dis-
rupted by conflict (the context) and a head nurse who comes in
to **work** on the evening shift so that she might **assess** what is

going on (strategic actions taken in response to interrupted work flow).

Consequences

Action and interaction taken in response to, or to manage, a phenomenon have certain *outcomes* or *consequences*. These might not always be predictable or what was intended. The failure to take action/interaction also has outcomes or *consequences*. Tracing out these consequences is also important in grounded theory.

There may be consequences to people, places, or things. Consequences may be events or happenings, such as an illness becoming worse due to the failure to follow a regimen. Or they may take the form of responsive actions/interactions, as when someone demands you do something, your counter strategy is to do it poorly or not at all. Consequences may be actual or potential, happen in the present or in the future. The consequences of one set of actions may become part of the conditions (as context or intervening ones) affecting the next set of action/interactions occurring in a sequence—or even part of conditions that follow in still another sequence. Therefore, what are **consequences of action/interaction at one point in time may become part of the conditions in another.**

Now to complete our situation of pain due to a broken leg, we can say one of the consequences of taking action to alleviate the pain is relief (a subcategory). Pain relief will also have its list of properties, as we said earlier, which for this specific situation can be located along a dimensional range. In our example of the broken leg, if we were out in the woods and with friends, and they, having some first aid training, put the leg in alignment, splinted it, and went for help, a consequence of these pain management strategies might be reduced pain. However, if the person happened to be alone and had to wait for someone to come along, there might be no pain relief. In fact, if someone didn't come along soon, the person potentially might go into shock from the pain and stress to the body. An increase in intensity and/or going into shock may affect the pain management strategies taken in the next action sequence, say when the person is found.

Linking and Developing Categories
By Means of the Paradigm

The linking and development of categories takes place through the basic analytic procedures introduced in Chapter 5, namely the asking of questions and the making of comparisons. The actual process of axial coding through these procedures is quite complex. It is complex because the analysis is, in fact, performing four distinct analytic steps almost simultaneously. These are: (a) the *hypothetical relating of subcategories to a category by means of statements denoting the nature of the relationships between them and the phenomenon*—causal conditions, context, intervening conditions, action/interactional strategies, consequences; (b) the *verification* of those hypotheses against actual data; (c) the *continued search for the properties* of categories and subcategories, and the *dimensional locations* of data (events, happenings, etc.) indicative of them; (d) the beginning exploration of *variation* in phenomena, by comparing each category and its subcategories for different patterns discovered by comparing dimensional locations of instances of data. In axial coding, the comparisons that one makes, and the questions that one asks, pertain to those steps listed above.

Relating Subcategories to a Category

In axial coding the nature of the questions we are asking are really questions denoting a type of relationship. For example, as we compare one category against another, we might pose the question: Is the category **Pain Relief** related to that of **Pain** as consequence of strategies taken to relieve that pain? Notice here, we are not talking about specific incidents or events that are coded, nor about specific properties or dimensions. Rather we are posing questions in terms of the conceptual labels themselves, and how one category might be related to another. If we saw that people with arthritis used certain strategies to relieve their pain, we might pose the question: Under conditions of Pain, what strategies do they use for Pain Management?, thereby relating the two categories.

Verification of Statements Against Data

With such category relating questions in mind, we then return to our data and look for evidence, incidents, and events that support or refute our questions. We look at each of our interviews, documents, and so forth, and check to see what people with arthritis do when they have pain. If our questions are supported by data, then we can change the question to a statement of relationship, a kind of hypothesis, and say: Under conditions of pain, arthritics use strategies for Pain Management. And: When arthritics use management strategies then they obtain Pain Relief. Notice that there is no specificity to these statements for they are just broad general statements.

At the same time that we are looking for evidence in the data to verify our statements of relationship, we are also looking for instances of when they might not hold up. We would expect in every interview or document that we examined, in which a person complains of having arthritic pain, that he or she would in fact do something about it and that the doing something would bring about relief. But doing something and obtaining relief are not unqualified statements. In other words, some persons may do nothing, yet obtain relief. Some might wait a while, others might do something in anticipation of pain. Others might wait so long to do something that when they do, they do not obtain pain relief. All of these instances qualify our original questions and statements of relationship. **They don't**

necessarily negate our questions or statements, or disprove them, rather **they add variation and depth of understanding.** It is just as important in doing grounded theory studies to find evidence of differences and variation, as it is to find evidence that supports our original questions and statements. The negative or alternative cases tell us that something about this instance is different, and so we must move in and take a close look at what this might be. **Following through on these differences adds density and variation to our theory.**

Further Development of Categories and Subcategories In Terms of Their Properties and Dimensional Locations

While we are examining our data, looking for evidence to support our questions and statements of relationships, and alternatives to these, we continue to watch for evidence of other properties of categories and the dimensional location of each incident that we code. For example, in regard to the subcategory of pain relief, we would want to know what other properties exist besides the ones we have already uncovered during open coding. And as we compare each incident, we want to know where each property can be dimensionally located. Again we are aiming for specificity, trying to locate and specify each incident of data in terms of exact dimensional location. Doing so gives our theory conceptual density and helps us to uncover as much variation as possible. A note of caution! The researcher has a responsibility to establish a balance between developing enough density and overdoing attempts to develop density. (See Chapter 11 on Theoretical Sampling.) One could continue this analytic process indefinitely. The idea is to have a theory that is conceptually dense and that has specificity, plus enough theoretical variation to enable it to be applied to many different instances of any given phenomenon.

Linking Categories at the Dimensional Level

Later when discussing selective coding (Chapter 8) we will show how one links together all of the major categories (remember we may have five or six categories, each developed in terms of its subcategories). But, it is here in axial coding that the process of linkage actually begins. While we do our analysis, we note patterns in our data in terms of dimensional locations of events, incidents pertaining to the property of a phenomenon. In other words, we notice differences between the way persons with intense pain of long duration manage as opposed to those with mild pain of short duration. Or differences in pain relief when pain relief measures (strategies to relieve pain) are taken in anticipation of pain, or when the pain trajectory first begins, as opposed to when measures are taken only later and the pain has gone on for some time. Looking for and noting these patterns are very important and provide the foundation for selective coding.

To complicate the picture, let us add the following. As you work with data, you will notice how clusters of specific properties of conditions, strategies, and outcomes pertaining to phenomenon interact with each other to bring about still other differences. For example, you might note that when pain is intense and of long duration then pain relief measures do not work, and that, with time, having discovered this, individuals might modify their strategies to implement pain measures earlier in the pain trajectory and this time obtain better results. Such changes indicate process or movement in the data. Though the concept of process will be taken up later in Chapter 9, it is important to note such changes early.

Complexity

If these procedures, techniques, and steps in axial coding seem overwhelmingly complicated, remember that reality, alas, is complex. Also, when you are actually coding data much of what was described above happens automatically. It is important to recognize what you are doing procedurally so that you can do it purposefully. In developing a grounded theory we are trying to capture as much of the complexity and movement in the real world that is possible, while knowing we are never able to grasp all of it. Recall, that we are not counting numbers, though we are looking for evidence to support and qualify our statements of relationships regarding the data. **The discovery and specification of differences among and within categories, as well as similarities, is crucially important and at the heart of grounded theory.**

Moving Between Inductive and Deductive Thinking

As you have probably noticed, while coding we are constantly moving between inductive and deductive thinking. That is, we deductively propose statements of relationships or suggest possible properties and their dimensions when working with data, then actually attempt to verify what we have deduced against data as we compare incident with incident. There is a **constant interplay between proposing and checking.** This back and forth movement is what makes our theory grounded!

For example, while coding, we might see an incident of pain management and propose that conditions of intense pain will be followed by measures taken to relieve pain. We then check each incident of intense pain that we come across in the data to determine if this is so, verifying inductively what we proposed deductively. Or we might be reading an interview and come across a statement such as "when I get up in the morning (condition) and my joints are stiff and painful (phenomenon), I sit on the edge of the bed before getting up and move each joint slowly and carefully (strategies). Then, when I do get up, movement is less awkward and less painful" (consequences). Here, the conditions, strategies, and consequences are spelled out for us. We noted them in the data themselves. However, one incident is not enough to confirm a set of relationships, or properties, or dimensions. Rather **our proposed relationships have to be supported over and over again in the data**, though the particulars may differ. That is, someone might say: "Before I go out shopping and do a lot of walking around" rather than, "When I get up in the morning." Or, rather than "moving joints slowly," "I take aspirin to minimize the pain." Going out shopping is another example of a condition that brings about pain, while taking aspirin is a preventative strategy for managing it. However, the specific incidents differ.

Concepts and relationships arrived at through deductive thinking must be verified over and over again against actual data. Initially they are held as provisional and if not supported they are discarded. **Your final theory is limited to those categories, their properties and dimensions, and statements of relationships that exist in the actual data collected**—not what you think might be out there but haven't come across. We are building grounded theory, and it is the purposeful grounding or verification process that makes this mode of theory building different from many other modes of theory building. This doesn't mean you can't also quantitatively test those relationships later or even now, but that in building theory you gather sufficient data to repeatedly give evidence of your categories and the relationships between them. What you can't find in your data becomes one of the limitations in your study. That is, either you didn't collect enough information, go to the right places, persons, and so forth. Or perhaps, your statements of relationships are not quite correct and need revision to fit the data at hand.

Tracking Down Relationships

Sometimes while coding you will come across what appears to be a strategy, condition, or consequence. If you identify an incident or event as such, you can trace back through the data to locate the phenomenon to which it seems to pertain, and other conditions that seem to be relevant to this situation. Also you can discover what strategies besides this one are being used and with what consequences. Purposefully tracking down relationships rather than waiting to stumble upon them in data makes your analysis more systematic, also it proceeds more quickly.

The Use of Miniframeworks and Other Recording Techniques

By now you are probably wondering just how do you keep track of all the products of your analysis! Without going into the details of memos and diagrams that will be discussed in Chapter 12, here are a few preliminary suggestions.

One technique for keeping track of one's analysis is the use of *miniframeworks*. These are sometimes very complex diagrams, in which one shows the crosscuts or ways in which subcategories interact with each other, and the category to which they are related. An example of this would be:

Phase 1	
Pain	*Phenomenon*
unknown cause	
new type	
intense	*Specific Properties*
brief duration	that determine
repeated	*Pain Management Context*
at fairly long intervals	
in one part of the body	
you assess → decided to "wait it out" will probably go away (based on past experience)	*Strategy for Management*
Phase 2	
Pain returns	*Phenomenon*
all of above properties	
you reassess and decide to take aspirin	*Strategy for Management*

Phase 3
Pain returns again   *Phenomenon*
less intense   *Specific Properties*
at longer intervals   that determine
                                         Pain Management Context
   You assess and take less aspirin   *Strategy*

Phase 4
Pain returns once more   *Phenomenon*
very intense   *Specific Properties*
spreads to other parts of body   that determine
lasts longer   *Pain Management Context*
   You reassess → Go to Physician. His   *Strategies*
                  or her technical as-
                  sessment (including
                  tests). Operation!

Another technique is to use the *logic diagrams* as we did throughout this chapter and fill in the relationships, properties, and dimensional ranges as you go along.

Then too, you can simply state the relationships in a *memo*, perhaps in capital and bold lettering, along with examples (typed below and in small lettering) from the data that either led to that statement of relationships or gave evidence to support it.

Summary

Axial coding is the process of relating subcategories to a category. It is a complex process of inductive and deductive thinking involving several steps. These are accomplished, as with open coding, by making comparisons and asking questions. However, in axial coding the use of these procedures is more focused, and geared toward discovering and relating categories in terms of the paradigm model. That is, we develop each category (phenomenon) in terms of the causal conditions that give rise to it, the specific dimensional location of this phenomenon in terms of its properties, the context, the action/interactional strategies used to handle, manage, respond to this phenomenon in light of that context, and the consequences of any action/interaction that is taken. Furthermore, in axial coding we continue to look for additional properties of each category, and to note the dimensional location of each incident, happening, or event.

We suggest that those of you who are only interested in, or whose projects involve, theme analysis or concept development might consider stopping your reading of the book here. You will have probably absorbed enough of grounded theory procedure for those alternative purposes. If you are concerned with developing a theory, read on!

8

Selective Coding

Definition of Terms

Story: A descriptive narrative about the central phenomenon of the study.

Story Line: The conceptualization of the story. This is the core category.

Selective Coding: The process of selecting the core category, systematically relating it to other categories, validating those relationships, and filling in categories that need further refinement and development.

Core Category: The central phenomenon around which all the other categories are integrated.

After some time (probably months) of collecting and analyzing data, you are now confronted with the task of integrating your categories to form a grounded theory! We have ended that sentence with an exclamation mark to vividly express the perplexity experienced by many researchers upon arriving at this point in their studies. Integrating one's materials is a task that even seasoned researchers find difficult.

As Paul Atkinson, a coauthor of an excellent textbook on field research (Hammersley & Atkinson, 1983) wrote in a personal communication:

> This aspect—making it all come together—is one of the most difficult things of all, isn't it? Quite apart from actually achieving it, it is hard to inject the right mix of (a) faith that it can and will be achieved; (b) recognition that it has to be worked at, and isn't based on romantic inspiration; (c) that it isn't like a solution to a puzzle or a math problem, but has to be created, (d) that you can't always pack everything into one version, and that any one project could yield several different ways of bringing it together.

As Atkinson implies, final integration is a complicated process but of course it can be done. In this chapter we will offer some guidelines for helping you to make that final leap between creating a list of concepts and producing a theory. **Integration is not much different than axial coding. It is just done at a higher more abstract level of analysis.**

In axial coding you developed the basis for selective coding. You now have categories worked out in terms of their salient properties, dimensions, and associated paradigmatic relationships, giving the categories richness and density. You should also have begun to note possible relationships between major categories along the lines of their properties and dimensions. Furthermore, you have probably begun to formulate some conception of what your research is all about. After all, people have been asking you for some months: What is it that you are studying, and what are your findings? Surely, some conclusion has formed in your mind, if not on paper. The question is: How do you take that which is in a rough form, and hopefully in your diagrams and memos (see Chapter 12 for these), and systematically develop it into a picture of reality that is conceptual, comprehensible, and above all grounded?

There are several steps through which this is accomplished. The first step involves explicating the *story line.* The second consists of *relating subsidiary categories* around the *core category* by means of the *paradigm*. The third involves *relating categories at the dimensional level*. The fourth entails *validating those relationships* against data. The fifth and final step consists of *filling in categories* that may need further refinement and/or development. It is important to understand here that these steps are not necessarily taken in linear sequence nor are they distinct in actual practice. It is only for explanatory purposes that we distinguish between them. **In reality one moves back and forth between them.**

In order to assist with comprehension of the integration process, data from a study carried out by one of the authors (Corbin) will be used to illustrate these procedural steps. As you will see, the study is relatively uncomplicated and straightforward. It focused on the issue of how 20 women with chronic illness managed their pregnancies. They were enlisted as subjects at the end of the first or beginning of the second trimester, and followed until six weeks after delivery. Four to five structured interviews were scheduled with each woman. One interview was scheduled for each trimester of the pregnancy, one within a week of the delivery, and the final one at six weeks after delivery. In addition, the investigator made observations during each prenatal visit and carried out informal interviews with the women at those times. If spouses were present during the interviews or observations, they too were observed and interviewed. Whenever feasible, the investigator also accompanied the women to any special pregnancy testing procedures that they may have undergone. A variety of illnesses were represented including diabetes, heart disease, lupus erythematosus, kidney disease, and hypertension. Some women had a combination of chronic conditions, such as diabetes and kidney disease. One woman had a kidney transplant. We should add that the researcher began her study with a general interest in what difference a chronic illness might make in heightening the risk of pregnancy. She had no conception that the women themselves played such an active role in managing pregnancy risks. Beginning to understand this, her perspective shifted from a medical-clinical one to that of a more open and less biased researcher (Corbin, 1987).

Explicating the Story Line

To achieve integration, it is necessary first to formulate and commit yourself to a story line. This is (see definition above) the conceptualization of a descriptive story about the central phenomenon of the study. (When analyzed it will become the core category.) **Sometimes making a commitment to a story line is difficult because one is so steeped in the data that everything seems important, or more than a single phenomenon seems salient.** We will discuss below procedures for arriving at your commitment. Remember the basic techniques of making comparisons and asking questions about the data.

Identifying the Story

One way to begin integrating is to sit down at the word process or typewriter, or with pencil and paper, and write in a few sentences the essence of your *story*. Ask yourself, what about this area of study seems most striking? What do I think is the main problem? Restricting your response to **just a few sentences** is important, for detail here would only confuse the issue. You simply want a **general descriptive overview** of the story. To use the example of the chronically ill pregnant women, when it came time to integrate the categories, the investigator wrote a memo that looked like this:

> The main story seems to be about how women with pregnancies complicated by chronic illness manage the risks they perceive to be associated with their pregnancies. Each pregnancy/illness can be said to be on-course, indicating that the risks are being managed, or off-course, indicating that they are not. Women are managing the perceived risks in order to have a healthy baby. This

desired outcome seems to be the primary force motivating them to do whatever is necessary to minimize the risks. However, they are not passive recipients of care but play a very important role in the management process. They not only are responsible for monitoring their illnesses and pregnancies at home, but also make very active decisions about the regimens they are told to follow. In the latter case they consider the harm that might come to the baby from procedures like amniocentesis or from taking high doses of certain medications while pregnant. They carefully weigh the risks and make judgements about the right thing to do. If they think the doctor is wrong, then they do what they (the women) think should be done.

In this example, it was management of the "risks factors" associated with a pregnancy/illness that was seen as the primary issue. The motivation for playing such an active management role was an overwhelming desire for a healthy baby. The reason the investigator chose to focus on risk management was because this phenomenon came through strongly in each of the interviews and observations. Every woman spoke of wanting a healthy baby despite the risks and of a willingness to do what was necessary to achieve this goal.

Moving From Description to Conceptualization: The Story Line

It is helpful and probably necessary to use description (the "story") to get one's thought down on paper. Yet, once you are committed to a story then it is necessary to move beyond description to conceptualization; that is, to the *story line*. It is time to tell the story **analytically.** This means, just as with open and axial coding, that the central phenomenon has to be given a name (and as a category gradually be related to other categories). Here, you might first look at your list of categories to see if one of them is abstract enough to encompass all that has been described in the story. Sometimes you already have such

a category. It now becomes the *core category*. At other times no
single category seems broad enough to say it all, so what do you
do then? The answer is you must give the central phenomenon
a name.

In the illustration above, the investigator had many categories but none sufficiently broad to encompass the main idea
of risk managing to protect the developing fetus. Each category seemed to describe a part of but not the whole phenomena. After much thought, the term "Protective Governing" was
chosen as the core category. Governing: meaning, mothers taking action to have some control over the risks associated with
their pregnancies; protective: indicating that those actions were
shielding in nature. (It would have been interesting to find
negative cases—women who did not take protective action—
but none were found during this study.) The grammatical form
that the core category takes can vary. It can be a noun like
trajectory, work, awareness, or dying. It can also be a combined
adjective and participle like protective governing or, a participle and noun like Becoming a Mother, and Living with
Arthritis. The choice is up to the analyst. The only requirement
is that the conceptual label fit the story it represents.

Making a Choice Between Two or More
Salient Phenomena

Sometimes two phenomena in the data strike the investigator as being equally important or of interest. **It is essential,
however, to make a choice between them** in order to achieve
the tight integration and the dense development of categories required of a grounded theory. To fully develop two core
categories, then to integrate the two, and write about them
with clarity and precision is very difficult. This is so even for
the experienced writer and researcher. (Essentially he or she
would be developing and writing about two distinct but related theories.) **The way to handle this problem is to choose**

one phenomenon, relate the other category to it as a subsidiary category, then write it as a single theory. Then, in another
paper or monograph you can take up the second idea and do
the same.

As an example, in a study by the authors, two phenomena
emerged as significant. Each would have been interesting to
pursue and write about. One phenomenon was the course of a
chronic illness and its management by spouses. The other was
the impact of body failure on their biographies. When it came
time to integrate the study, we decided to focus on the illness
course and its management. Biography would be kept as a
secondary concept, this phenomenon acting both as a condition
to management and in turn affected by the management. In a
future publication, body failure and its impact upon biography
will be given primary focus. Then the chronic illness and its
management will be seen as a set of conditions affecting both
the degree of body failure and the management of biography in
relationship to that failure.

What If I Cannot Define the Story Line?

Sometimes researchers are also practitioners who are doing
research in the area of their practice. Then, they find it difficult to distance themselves from their materials sufficiently to
allow adequate description and conceptualization of the story
line, and thus to choose a core category. Here it helps to get
consultation from a more experienced researcher, teacher, or
colleague; someone who can listen, and help sort it all out. The
consultant can ask questions such as: What phenomena are
reflected over and over again in your data? Give me a summary
of your findings? What essential message about this research
area do you want to pass on to others? What do you consider
important about this area and why? (For an example of a
consultative session between a teacher and student see Strauss,
1987, p. 166.)

Determining the Properties and
Dimensions of the Core

Just like the other categories, the *core category* must become developed in terms of its properties. If you tell the story properly, in addition to revealing the core category **the story should also indicate its properties**.

Returning to the pregnancy illustration: Two major properties and their dimensions were identified. These were "perceived risks," which varied along the dimension of high to low. There were two sources of risks, the pregnancy and the illness, each complicating the other, and each following a course. The pregnancy and illness could each be said to be on course or proceeding the way it should because the risks were being contained; or off course, indicating that something was wrong because the risks factors were not being controlled. Graphed, the properties and their dimensional range look like this:

Property	Dimensional Range	
perceived risks	low	high
pregnancy-illness course	on	off

Once the properties of the core category are identified, the **next step is to relate the other categories to it**, thereby making them *subsidiary categories*. Before proceeding with our discussion, however, there are two questions about the core category that we should address.

The first is whether or not the core category must be a "basic psychosocial process" (Glaser, 1978, p. 100: See also Chapter 9, which discusses "process" in much detail). The answer is no. Grounded theory is an action oriented model, therefore in some way the theory has to show action and change, or the reasons for little or minimal change. But the core category itself does not have to be a process, much less a basic psychosocial one, though it certainly may be. (See also Chapter 11 on "process.")

Recollect from our discussion of the story line that a decision as to the central phenomenon is crucial to the study. **The central**

phenomenon is at the heart of the integration process. It is the
essential cement in putting together—and keeping together
properly—all the components in the theory. Once we have
determined the phenomenon and named it as a core category,
then we go through all the remaining procedural steps described in this chapter. But in the analysis it is the phenomenon
focused upon that is the researcher's core category.

For instance, the concept of "awareness" (Glaser & Strauss,
1965) is a noun that speaks to a special kind of phenomenon,
that is, different types of awareness in X setting. The book in
which the phenomenon is analyzed shows action and change,
bringing process in as well as all the elements of the paradigm.
It addresses how various types of awareness (context) come to
be (conditions for action/interaction), how they are maintained
(strategies), how they change (process), and what that means
for those involved (consequences). However, in the book itself,
awareness is the concept around which the book is organized.

The second question concerns criteria for choosing a core
category. The criteria should fit and describe the phenomenon
for what they stand. Also, the criteria must be broad enough to
encompass and relate, as subsidiary categories, the other categories. The core category must be the sun, standing in orderly
systematic relationships to its planets.

Relating Other Categories to the Core Category

Again, **the relating of categories to the core category is done
by means of the paradigm**—conditions, context, strategies,
consequences. As noted previously, the names given to categories may not necessarily include these paradigmatic terms. So,
the problem is to identify which category denotes what part of
the paradigm. This identification essentially orders them into
subcategories in paradigmatic relationship. Simplified, the analytic ordering looks something like this: A (conditions) leads
to B (phenomenon), which leads to C (context), which leads to

D (action/interaction, including strategies), which then leads to E (consequences).

Again, we will momentarily put aside the detail that goes with each subsidiary category and confine ourselves to working with the categories themselves. Remember that the actual relating of categories to each other is far more complex than a simple cause leads to consequence, because of the presence of intervening sets of conditions that enter at various points (see Chapters 7 and 10 for discussions of intervening conditions). It is these intervening conditions that explain why one person has a certain outcome or chooses a certain set of strategies while another person doesn't. Therefore it is essential to identify and relate these conditions to other categories.

Returning to the Story

How are categories to be arranged and rearranged in terms of their paradigmatic relationships, so as to adequately fit the story line? To show this, again we return to our story telling. Only this time we fill in a little more of the descriptive detail. Hence our story about pregnant women with chronic illness now looks like this:

Having a chronic condition changes the nature of pregnancy, adding an element of risk that would not otherwise be there. It is the interaction between illness and pregnancy that creates the **risks factors**. Twenty to thirty years ago, women with conditions such as diabetes, kidney disease, and lupus were very fortunate if they were able to deliver a live baby. Also, their own health by the time they reached childbearing age was in such jeopardy, that they were lucky to be able even to get and/or stay pregnant. Today, many chronic conditions can be treated and kept under control, tremendously improving the health of women during their childbearing years. While such pregnancies are still given special consideration, modern technology has really increased a woman's chances of delivering a live and healthy child, and provides a means of handling specific neonatal problems that might arise after the child is born. Naturally, the more severe the illness and the more difficult it is to keep symptoms under control, then the greater the associated risks. Also there are certain points in the pregnancy course that seem to the health personnel more dangerous than others. For instance, the thirty seventh week seems to be a turning point for diabetics, so monitoring by the health team intensifies after this time.

It is interesting to note how the women come to **define** the **risk level**. They gather data from a variety of cues. They look to cues from their doctors and nurses. But they also rely on their own and other's past experiences with the illness and with pregnancy. They are also alert to the fetus itself, interpreting its movements and its perceived growth read in terms of their own increasing size. They also **monitor** how they feel physically. All of this gives them data for estimating their level of risk.

Another important feature is that the women, as well as health team members, **weigh** the various risks associated with the different proposed treatments. They weigh the risks not only to the baby but to themselves and to others (**balancing**). If the women think that a certain dosage of a medication is too high or too low, such that it will harm the baby, then they will either negotiate with their doctors to change medication or change it themselves. Or, if they think that a treatment they are receiving is not correct, they will try to negotiate for a change in it. If unsuccessful with their negotiations, they will even leave the hospital against medical advice in order to save their baby and themselves. The women also weigh the risks of various regimens and treatments to their families' functioning. It is very difficult for a woman with two other small children to rest every afternoon. If she has no one to look after her children, then she may not rest.

Management is a joint function shared by the women and the health team. By entering the health care system, these women are delegating part of the management function to their physicians, that part which involves diagnosis and determination of treatment. The actual carrying out of treatment is done by the women (and spouse) at home, unless of course they need hospitalization. Their management strategies, like those of their physicians, are aimed at **controlling** the risks. Some of the strategies are for controlling the physical risks of harm to baby and self, some are to control psychological fear associated with the physical risks. The baby's father also plays a salient but less direct part in the management process. His is a more supportive role. Whenever possible, the fathers come with the mothers to the prenatal checkups. They are almost sure to be there if they can get off work, or when the woman is having a special procedure, needs to be hospitalized, or has other important decisions to make. The outcomes of the controlling strategies vary. If the illness and pregnancy are kept on course, the risks are contained, then the goal of a healthy baby is achieved. Sometimes the risks could not be contained. Despite the hard work of the health team and woman, the pregnancy was destabilized by the illness or the illness caused obstetrical complications. One baby died because of complications shortly after birth. Other babies were in the intensive care nursery for a while but were eventually discharged in good health. All the women believed their babies were really special because they had gone through so much to get them. Also, some couples felt the experience drew them closer together, because they had undergone so much together.

Using such a story as a guideline, the analyst can begin to **arrange and rearrange the categories in terms of the paradigm until they seem to fit the story, and to provide an analytic version of the story**. Otherwise the categories remain just a list of items. Here is an illustration of this ordering. In the pregnancy study, the categories that emerged included: Risks Factors (sources of risks), Risks Context, Desire for a Healthy Baby, Assessing, Balancing, Controlling (a joint management process), and Outcome (risk containment). There were two other salient categories. These became the properties of the core concept, **Protective Governing**, once it was identified. Recall, they were: **perceived risk level** and **pregnancy/illness course**.

Eventually Risks Factors (the interactive effect of pregnancy and illness) were seen as creating the risk *conditions* that led to the need for the special type of management termed Protective

Governing. The Risk Context was identified as the *context* leading to action. It denoted where along the risk continuum a
woman placed herself, and whether or not she saw her pregnancy and illness as proceeding along their respective courses.
Here, as in axial coding, Risk Context was created through the
interaction of the properties of Protective Governing. The context varied according to the range of *dimensions* or possible
combination of both perceived level of risk and pregnancy/ill-
ness course. Assessing (an action) was seen as a *condition inter-*
vening between the phenomenon of Protective Governing and
Risk Context. This is because assessments of cues became the
means by which women defined their pregnancies as risk levels. They had to gather information about their specific risk
factors, and the accuracy of information gathered was based
upon knowledge levels, previous pregnancy experience, interpretation of events that occurred during prenatal checkups, and
so forth.

Controlling became the term for the *strategies* women used
to manage both the physical and psychological risks that they
associated with their pregnancy. (Although controlling is a
management process involving both the health team and the
women, immediately below we will refer only to the women's
actions.) Motivation and balancing were seen as salient conditions intervening between risk context and controlling, because
treatment options were always balanced against their desire for
a healthy baby. (Built into this balancing of course were the
options open to them. That is, the technology available, their
physicians knowledge of it, plus many other intervening conditions such as experience with illness.) The controlling actions
were in essence the outcome of that balancing process. The
category of Outcome Risks Containment became equivalent to
the *consequences*, or the end result of those controlling strategies.
That is, keeping the pregnancy/illness risks factors contained,
which in the end lead to the healthy baby. Graphically, the
analytic diagram looked something like this:

Risk Factors Associated with a pregnancy + Chronic Illness →
leads to the Need for Protective Governing

How Protective Governing is Carried Out:
Assessing leads to Definition of Risk Contexts which modified
through: Motivation, Balancing, + Other Intervening Conditions → lead to F: Strategies for Controlling the Risks → which
then result in Risks Containment.

This ordering of categories was not arrived at without a great
deal of thought. Some of the placement of items was obvious;
for instance, there is no doubt that controlling is a strategy. The
placement of assessing and balancing were more difficult, however. They denote action without actually being strategies to
control outcome, though they affect it. Together, assessing,
balancing, and controlling can be viewed as the means by which
protective governing is actually carried out, a kind of three-step
process.

**The storytelling and its sequential order are the keys to
ordering the categories in a clear fashion.** If the story is told
accurately and logically, the ordering of categories should proceed without a great deal of difficulty.

Difficulty in Ordering the Categories

**If at a comparable point in your study you are still having
difficulty when relating your categories, then you should
rewrite or retell your story.** Difficulty in integrating implies
that something is wrong with or missing in the logic of your
story. You may have to rewrite it several times until you get it
right, so that the placement of categories makes sense to you.

Validating the Relationships

One could now write a hypothetical statement regarding relationships among the categories. Though rather complicated,
a statement about the pregnancy management might look this:
Under conditions of a pregnancy complicated by chronic illness, women take protective action to manage perceived risks

by means of assessing the risk level, balancing their treatment options, and using a joint management process—termed "controlling"—so that they might contain the risks and have a healthy baby. Armed with such a statement one can go back to the data or to the field to validate it. Does the statement hold in a broad sense for each of the persons in the study? In the actual research endeavor this was done, the statement held up in case after case. But notice something about the statement: It is very static and really doesn't explain any of the complexity and variation that the investigator was seeing. So now what? To answer this, we go to the next step in the integration process.

Uncovering the Patterns

During axial coding, one begins to notice certain "patterns" (repeated relationships between properties and dimensions of categories). For instance, it became obvious to the investigator in the pregnancy study that the womens' perceptions of risks tended to vary with the pregnancy and illness circumstances over the course of the pregnancy, and that as their perceptions changed so did their strategies.

Also in building categories during axial coding, a certain amount of integration naturally occurs. Take the category of Assessing, as an example. When we ask why the women are constantly assessing, we automatically respond with "because of the risks whose source is the combined effect of pregnancy and illness." Thus two categories, Assessing and Risk Factors, are related, even though in axial coding the proposed relationships are still quite loose.

In other words there is a web, a network of conceptual relationships already there, though somewhat loose and tangled, that the analyst will have to sort out and refine later during his or her selective coding. **It is very important to identify these patterns and to group the data accordingly, because this is what gives the theory specificity. One is then**

able to say: Under these conditions (listing them) this happens; whereas under these conditions, this is what occurs.

Systematizing and Solidifying Connections

To systematize and solidify connections we use a combination of inductive and deductive thinking, in which we constantly move between asking questions, generating hypotheses, and making comparisons.

From our discussion of coding so far, you know that the context is the specific set of properties of the phenomenon—the conditions—in which actions are embedded. You also know that the context is really an arrangement. An arrangement of what? Of the properties of the general phenomenon, ordered in various combinations, along their dimensional ranges **to form patterns.** (This latter statement is only an elaboration of the initial definition given and discussed in Chapter 7.)

To see how this works visually, let's go back to our example of Protective Governing. Its properties were identified as: "perceptions of risks," which can range from high to low, and pregnancy/illness "course", which can range from being on course to off course. These combine in various patterns to create the action context. In the pregnancy study, four contexts were identified. These were:

(1) The On-Course, Lower-Risk Context.
(2) The On-Course, Higher-Risk Context.
(3) The Off-Course, Noncritical Context.
(4) The Off-Course, Critical Context.

Ways in Which These Combinations Are Discovered

There are several ways one might discover these patterns. **The combinations may simply emerge during analysis.** After being immersed in the data for months one can't help but note differences or the emerging patterns. Perhaps the researcher does not immediately recognize all of the details of those patterns but does get a sense of difference. In the pregnancy study, the investigator noted that perceptions of risks tended to change over time according to the pregnancy and illness circumstances. Once theoretically sensitive to this change, the investigator looked to the data for further evidence of this patterning as well as the specifics of why, how, and so forth.

Or, once knowing the properties of the central phenomenon you can deduce the various combinations. A fourfold table works well for doing this:

Sometimes, you fortuitously come across the patterned differences. You notice something different in the data while coding and trace it back to make the discovery explicit. Or, while making an observation you have a sudden insight precipitated by your observations or by something said in an interview; the connections that you have been pondering for weeks become clear. The same may happen while you are talking with a colleague or doing pertinent reading, or even when driving down the street. This sudden insight and the "high" that often accompanies it are what grounded theorists often refer to as the "joy of discovery." (It's always wise to have a pencil and paper handy to jot down these bolts of analytic lightning; Glaser, 1978, p. 58). (We discussed this procedure under Axial Coding in Chapter 7.)

Grouping of Categories

Having identified the differences in context, the researcher can begin systematically to group the categories. **They are grouped along the dimensional ranges of their properties in accordance with discovered patterns. This grouping again is done by asking questions and making comparisons.** Return again to the study of the pregnant women and think of the category, Assessing. One of the properties of Assessing was that it was based on Cues. That is, the women looked to cues about the nature of the risk factors as judged pertinent by them. Cues in turn had a subproperty: type (of cue). Type was subdivided into physical, interactional, temporal, and objective cues. The question to be pursued in the data analysis at this point was: How did the cues vary according to the various contexts? To put it another way: How do physical, interactional, temporal, and objective cues differ between the low risks/on-course context, and the higher risk/on-course context? How in turn do the cues differ with the noncrisis/off-course context and the crisis/off-course context? Notice that we are actually comparing along the potential dimensional ranges. That is, interaction, temporal, physical, and objective cues should differ in type, intensity, and so forth. These differences allow us to match the cues to the various contexts.

In the pregnancy study, not only was Assessing analyzed in this fashion, but so were Risk Factors, Balancing, Controlling, and Outcomes. To aid in the analysis, the investigator asked the following questions. How did the illness and pregnancy risk factors differ for each of these contexts? What options were the women balancing in each context, and how did their desire for a healthy baby influence the decisions that they made? What form did joint management take in each context, in terms of controlling strategies? How did the outcomes of the strategies differ? By systematically examining the data in this fashion, the pieces of the analytical puzzle that inevitably confront a researcher begin to come together. **The data are now related not only at the broad conceptual level, but also at the property and dimensional levels for each major category.** You now have the rudiments of a theory!

Grounding the Theory

Validating one's theory against the data completes its grounding. One does this by laying out the theory in memos either diagrammatically or narratively. Then statements regarding the category relationships under varying contextual conditions are developed and finally validated against the data. Again, these procedures can usefully be described by using data from the pregnancy study.

Laying Out the Theory

If one were to narratively lay out the theory of Protective Governing, at this point, it would look something like the following. (Much detail has been omitted.)

Protective Governing Under Conditions of an On-Course Lower-Risk Context

Risks are assessed to be relatively low, and pregnancy and illness are perceived to be proceeding on course because the courses of risks—the illness and pregnancy—are stable. The **Physical, Interactional, Temporal, and Objective Cues** that led women to this **Assessment** included: few and/or mild physical symptoms of illness, medical test results were within a "normal" range, baby's heartbeat and growth were normal, and there was fetal movement. The women felt "healthy" and believed they had "illness under control." Most were in the early part of the pregnancy. As a result of their assessment, all of the women concluded that the **Problem** they faced was to keep the risk contained and illness and pregnancy on course.

In terms of **Balancing**, they saw themselves as **Having a Choice** when it came to treatment options. Some were able to discontinue taking risk-posing medications at this time, others at least could lower the dosages. Other treatments—such as rest and diet—were seen as flexible. The women did what was necessary within limits of their own tolerance and their family's functioning.

Joint management in this context may be described as Adjunctive Control; that is, a shared responsibility between the women and the health team. The women perceived the role of the health team as being that of **Assistant Support**. The stability of the illness/pregnancy and a woman's self-confidence in her ability to manage were among the important intervening conditions enabling this type of management. The health team's controlling strategies may be described as **Overseeing the Well-Being of the Woman and the Fetus**. The team's overseeing was often carried out **Within Restraints** due to the busy schedule of the physicians and because these pregnancies were not so demanding of the personnel's time and energy. The women's controlling strategies may be described as **Investing in a Healthy Baby and Self**. This type of controlling was carried out through several tactics. For instance, the women adhered more strictly to their medical regimens than when not pregnant. Because many were already taking medications to control their illnesses, they were especially careful to avoid potentially teratogenic substances, such as coffee and alcohol. They stopped taking over-the-counter drugs such as aspirin, preferring to put up with the discomforts of a headache. They improved their diets by eating more vegetables and increasing their protein intake. Doing all of this required some adjustments at home, but most women found their families cooperative. The women became especially watchful, often negotiating with the physician to cut down on drug dosages, offering to rest more, and so forth, if the physician thought this would help. The spouse's controlling strategy in this context was described as **Watching Over His Investment**. Spouses' tactics included reminding the women to stay on their regimens, praising them for their efforts, and participating in gathering information about the special needs attending the pregnancy.

The women had few psychological fears, **Consequential Concerns**, about outcome as long as they stayed within this context of low-risk, on course. They attended prenatal classes, named their baby, imagined its appearance, bought clothes, and selected furniture. In order to alleviate any potential fears that they might have, they used positive thinking and imagery.

There were times when **Risk Perceptions Differed** between the women and health team, the women assessing the risks to be higher or lower than those assessed by the health team. When this happened, each party used strategies and counter strategies in an attempt to convince the other. Sometimes they

were successful but at other times they were not (for analytically specifiable reasons). Yet it was the respective parties'
perceptions of risks that guided their actions, whether the other
party agreed or not.

When controlling efforts were successful, the risks were
contained, and the pregnancy and illness kept on course. The
Payoff for their efforts was the Risk Containment and the
Outcome of a "healthy" baby and mother. The women had the
vaginal deliveries they had hoped for. They were willing also
to take the chance of another pregnancy. Right after delivery
and six weeks later, the women evinced strong attachment to
their infants.

This low-risk/on-course context is in distinct contrast to another that is described next to show the differences analytically.

The Off-Course, Noncritical Context

Risks were assessed to be high and the pregnancy/illness off
course because something had gone wrong with the illness or
pregnancy. One, or both was no longer stable. Medical or obstetrical complications threatened the outcome, but had not yet
reached crisis proportions. Cues that led the women to this
Assessment included: An increase in medical symptoms, such
as difficulty in breathing or fatigue so that even routine activities became troublesome. Other cues were the development
of obstetrical complications, such as premature labor, bleed-
ing, and preeclampsial. Or, a woman was told that her baby's
growth was inadequate, that it was "small for gestational age."
Or when the thirty-seventh week was reached, the health care
team stepped up its monitoring efforts including the use of
additional obstetrical tests. Yet there were positive signs reassuring the women that they still had a chance to birth a healthy
baby. Strong fetal heart tones and a normal amount of fetal
movement were among the reassuring cues. The **Problem** as
they saw it now was to bring the illness/pregnancy under
control, and to set it back on course in order to contain the risks.

The women were still highly motivated by their desire to have a healthy baby. **Balancing** at this time was more complicated because they had fewer treatment options from which to choose. They had to make **Trade-offs.** Sometimes saving the pregnancy meant taking a medication that had potential side effects. It was a matter of choosing the medication that had the lowest risk. Also, having to be hospitalized often meant risks to job, the schooling of other children, and so forth. Here too the women had to choose between the anticipated baby's welfare and that of job and family. Though the baby was given priority, the decision to put it first was often a difficult one.

Joint management under these conditions was termed **Entrusted Control**. The instability of the illness and/or pregnancy and the women's confidence that the health team could contain the risks were the intervening conditions that enabled this type of control. The health team responded by **Increasing their Controlling Efforts**, with such tactics as seeing the woman more often, conferring with other physicians, increasing the obstetrical and medical tests, changing treatment modes, and often using hospitalization in order to gain greater control over management. The women's controlling strategies at this time were termed **Taking the Necessary Measures**. They increased their monitoring of symptoms, reporting all change to their physicians. They modified their activities as necessary, even if it meant temporary hospitalization or moving in with family members who could take care of them. Medical regimens were strictly adhered to. The situation at home often put restraints on their management efforts. If a woman could find no one to care for her other young offspring, then she couldn't be hospitalized but had to do her best at home. Viewed medically, the hospitalizations were seen as desirable but under these conditions would be disruptive to home life. The women used telephones to keep the lines of communication open between hospital and home.

In three cases, the women felt that the treatments they were receiving in the hospital were actually increasing the risks to baby and self. When negotiation failed to result in a change of treatment, they resorted to the strategy of **Retaking Delegated Control** by leaving the hospital "to save their babies" and themselves.

The spouses' management efforts in this particular context were termed **Becoming a Temporary Caretaker**. They not only had to provide extra support to pregnant partners but also temporarily to take over what were normally the women's domestic chores at home. **Consequential Concerns** tended to increase in this context. Fearful that they might not have a healthy baby, the women used the protective strategy of **Holding Back** on making preparations for their baby until the risks were contained.

When management efforts were successful, the pregnancy/illness was put back on course and the risks contained, thus enabling the women to reach their desired **Outcomes**. The birth of a healthy baby was seen as a **Fantastic Relief**. There were both vaginal and Caesarean deliveries. Two infants were small for gestational age. Some women chose to keep open their options for future pregnancies and others decided that the risks were too great. Though some women held back from making emotional and physical preparations for the baby during the pregnancy, all showed positive attachment after the baby was born.

Making and Validating Statements of Relationships

With the various aspects of the **theory** thus **laid out in memo form**, either graphically or narratively, the analyst is ready **to make statements of relationship and to validate these statements with the data**. There should be statements denoting the relationships between each of the above categories, as they varied according to context. These relationships can be compared against the data, both to verify the statement and to support the differences between the contexts at the dimensional level.

For example one might make such statements as: **When** these . . . interactional, objective, temporal, and physical cues are present, then the women will assess their pregnancy to be of lower risk and on course. **Under conditions** that a woman perceives her pregnancy to be of lower risk and on course, and if she is highly motivated to have a healthy baby, **then** she will use a form of joint management that can be described as Adjunctive Management. **If** adjunctive management is successful, and the risks are contained, **then** the women will deliver healthy babies.

One could also make these statements: **When** women perceive their pregnancy to be of lower risk and on course, **then** they will make preparations for the baby. Or, **when** women perceive their pregnancy to be off course, though noncritical, **then** they will delay making preparations for the baby until the risks are contained.

Such statements are then checked against each case to determine whether or not they fit. **Again, one is looking to see if they fit in a general sense and in most cases, not necessarily in every single case exactly**. Continuing modifications and changes can be made in the statements until a general match is made.

What If a Case Does Not Fit the Theory?

Occasionally one comes across a prototypical case, one that fits the pattern exactly. However, usually there isn't a perfect fit. One tries to place cases in the most appropriate context, using the criterion of **best** rather than exact fit. But one doesn't force a match. There are cases that do not seem to belong anywhere. There are reasons for this.

Some cases represent a **state of transition** because some change has occurred or is occurring in the basic conditions leading to the central phenomenon. This change of conditions in turn changes the properties along their dimensions and the context leading to action. When in a state of change or transition, cases may exhibit aspects of two different contexts. They lie somewhere in the middle, not really fitting either. One way to account for this difference is to bring process into the theory. (This will be discussed in Chapter 10.)

Another explanation for a case that doesn't fit anywhere is that **intervening conditions** often come into play. For example, it is possible that a woman might feel that staying in bed for nine months is more than she is willing to do to have a healthy baby. She might choose a form of governing that is less protective to her fetus but more protective to her other interests. This doesn't necessarily negate the theory of protective governing, or statements of relationship between categories. Rather, again it denotes variation. The analyst must now **trace back and try to determine what conditions are causing this particular variation**. Once identified, these can be built into the theory.

For example, look back to the example above of the On-Course/Lower-Risk Context. Notice that there is a category termed **When Perceptions Differ**. Under the Off-Course/Noncritical Context, there is another category named **Taking Back Control**. These categories were built in to explain variations in Joint Management. When in an On-Course, Lower-Risk Context, and the women perceived the risks levels to be lower than those perceived by health practitioners, then they did not follow the prescribed regimens. Instead they made their own decisions about what was necessary to do or not to do. When they were in an Off-Course/Noncritical Context, the women used a form of joint management—entrusted control—meaning that they turned over much of the management to the health practitioners, usually by accepting hospitalization as a form of treatment. However, if they thought that the treatment was actually harmful then they took back the control, usually by leaving the hospital.

Still another point to be made is that **individual cases have to be broken up into respective pieces**. This is especially true if done in a series or over time, and even if scattered over several interviews or observations. For example, in the pregnancy study, because risk levels sometimes changed drastically, even over a period of a few days in response to changes in the illness/pregnancy status, one interview might contain data pertinent to two or more contexts. Or at one moment a mother-to-be might talk about entrusting control, while at the next she is relating how she retook control, sometimes jumping back and forth between the two. The analyst has to sort out these respective pieces and not treat any one case or interview as a single entity. Remember we analyze incidents, events, happenings, not cases as such.

Filling in the Gaps in Categories

Satisfied that the theoretical framework holds up to scrutiny and that conditions and processes are built in and accounted for, **the analyst can then go back to the categories and fill in any missing detail.** This is necessary to give *conceptual density* to the theory, as well as to add increased *conceptual specificity*. Usually this filling-in continues even through the project phase of writing for publication, since the writing itself reveals occasional minor gaps in the theoretical formulation. (We discuss this point further in Chapter 13.)

For example, suppose in the pregnancy study that after the data had been classified into specific patterns of risks context, the investigator then found that the categories and dimensions pertaining to the Lower-Risk, On-Course Context were well developed. In contrast, those pertaining to the Higher-Risk, On-Course Context were poorly developed. Given this situation, the analyst can return to the field and specifically collect data to fill the gaps in the theoretical formulation. This process of filling in can be done with any category that seems poorly developed.

This concludes our discussion of selective coding. But we remind you again that the five procedures around which this chapter was organized are not to be used in lockstep sequential order. We had to write about them in sequence so that you could better understand each set of analytic procedures. When you are experienced in using them, then you will scarcely notice how you move back and forth between them.

Summary

Integrating all the interpretive work done over the course of one's research is perhaps the most difficult task. Even experienced researchers may struggle with this. Grounded theory procedures help measurably with integration. In this chapter we have reviewed the functions of getting the story straight, developing a clear story line, and translating these into an *analytic* story. Central to the procedures is the selection of a core category and the relating of all major categories both to it and to each other. We have also illustrated how this is done with an extended case illustration.

9

Process
Definition of Terms

Process: The linking of action/interactional sequences.

Contingency: An unanticipated/unplanned happening that brings about a change in conditions.

Bringing process into the analysis is an important part of any grounded theory study. By process we mean the linking of sequences of action/interaction as they pertain to the management of, control over, or response to, a phenomenon. **This linking of sequences is accomplished by noting**: (a) the change in conditions influencing action/interaction over time; (b) the action/interactional response to that change; (c) the consequences that result from that action/interactional response; and finally by (d) describing how those consequences become part of the conditions influencing the next action/ interactional sequence. Change can be the consequence of planned action/interaction or it may occur as a result of *contingency*, an unanticipated and unplanned for happening that brings about change in conditions.

"Process" is an elusive term, one that is not easily explained. It doesn't necessarily stand out as such in data. Nor, does its discovery entail a specific set of procedures as those discussed in Chapters 5, 6, 7, and 8. Yet process is very much there in data, a part of any empirical reality. One knows if it's there, feels its presence as changed action/interaction, even though one can't actually see it as such.

Though a difficult idea for the beginning analyst to grasp, process is a very powerful analytic notion. For it is the conceptualization of events captured by the term **process** that explains why action/interactional routines break down, why problems occur in the course of life events, and why when looking back at life one sees growth, development, movement; or at the other extreme, the failure of growth, a sliding backwards, stagnation. (The latter represent a failure of response to a change in conditions, which is just as important to understand as is response).

Process in Grounded Theory

The grounded theory that evolves when process is built into analysis is a dynamic one. Process is a way of giving life to data by taking snapshots of action/interaction and linking them to form a sequence or series (Figure 9.1).

To capture process analytically, one must show the evolving nature of events by noting why and how action/interaction—in the form of events, doings, or happenings—will change, stay the same, or regress; why there is progression of events or what enables continuity of a line of action/interaction, in the face of changing conditions, and with what consequences.

A question that might come to mind while reading what we are about to say is: If one does the grounded theory analysis as one has been taught to do in previous chapters—tracing out conditions, actions, consequences—shouldn't process just naturally emerge? The response to that question is: It should! But unless the analyst is made keenly aware of the need to identify process, to build it into analysis, it is often omitted or done in a very narrow and limited fashion. Analysts may talk about

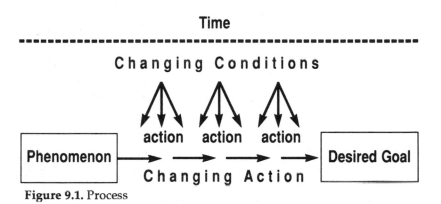

Figure 9.1. Process

steps or phases occurring in phenomena without accounting for or explaining variation in rate of movement, or why a passage upward might reverse itself or be interpreted and with what consequences.

To grasp what we mean by process over and above the usual way of handling it in studies, consider the following examples.

Scenario 1

You have a free afternoon and decide to catch up on your journal reading. You come across an article that catches your attention. The research is about management styles. It says there are three basic types of managers: the involved manager, the detached manager, and the controlling manager. It tells you in detail the conditions under which you might find each type of manager, gives a description of the interactional strategies that they use, and lists some of the consequences of each style of management upon the work situation. The article goes on to state that management styles are not fixed, rather people often change styles, choosing that which seems most appropriate at the time.

Analysis. This article hints at process. It tells us that managers do change styles. But it fails to follow through because it doesn't tell us what happens to change a controlling manager into an involved manager. Or, what is going on that leads an involved manager to become a detached one? Or, how a controlling manager can maintain this stance in the face of changing work situations. For instance, if and when the controlling manager meets someone who is not about to be controlled, yet the manager needs this person because he or she is the only one around with the skills necessary to accomplish an important job, so can't fire him or her: What does the controlling manager do under these conditions?

Scenario 2

You come across another report that catches your eye. This one is titled "Moving Up the Corporate Ladder." It details the steps that a manager passes through as he or she moves from lower levels to higher levels of management within an organization, along with some of the personal and organizational conditions that promote that movement, the strategies that are used to move one along, and some of the consequences.

Analysis. This article is an improvement on the one discussed before it, in terms of bringing process into the picture. It does show movement, progress, and explains what brings it about. What is missing, you ask? It's not complete, for it fails to take variation into account. It implies without meaning to that there is regularity of the steps or universal invariance of conditions, thereby rigidifying what is supposed to be process. Or gives a model of the ideal progression, without showing how that ideal varies by context. For example, pertaining to Scenario 2, one still might ask: Does everyone move through the steps at the same pace? Is it slower for some, faster for others? Why? Does everyone who starts off on the corporate trail move to the top? If not, why not? Where do they stop, slide backwards, and why? What critical factors come into play and when to prevent, hinder, halt their forward progression? How does a change in context by place and time affect rate and degree of progress?

Scenario 3

You come across a third article. It's about work in organizations and the division of labor that pertains to this work. Since you are studying work, you read on. It explains the many types of work to be done in the organization being studied, details who is assigned that work, and explains how the assigned persons carry it out, and some of the consequences.

Analysis. A rather static picture of work in organizations, don't you think? To give it life, to bring process into the picture, what would one want to know? Are the lines in the division of labor rigid or are they flexible? Do the lines of work ever overlap? Are there conditions under which one person or group might do another's assigned or designated tasks? What happens as a result? For example, might a nurse working in an emergency room or an intensive care unit perform tasks that are normally designated to or belong within the domain of physicians under other less medically intense conditions? Might a head nurse or supervisor, who normally does administrative tasks, take over and do the work of staff nursing during a strike?

Process—It Is a Matter of Degree

As you can probably guess by now, our conception of process is more than a cursory allusion to change, or a simple description of phases or stages. It involves an in-depth examination of and incorporation of changed action/interaction into analysis, as this varies over time in response to changes in conditions.

Just how much process is it necessary to account for in your analysis? That depends upon the research situation, also your time, energy, and experience as a researcher. Realistically, you could never capture all of the change and movement that occurs in reality. It would be too overwhelming. On the other hand, **process must be accounted for to a degree sufficient to give the reader a sense of the flow of events that occur with the passage of time.**

Inductive and Deductive Thinking

As with any aspect of analysis discussed in this book, deductive as well as inductive thinking are both very much a part of the analytic process. For instance, there may be times when the analyst is not able immediately to find evidence of process in the data. Either it's there, but not recognized as such; or there is insufficient data to bring it out. When this happens, the analyst can turn to deductive thinking and hypothesize possible potential situations of change, then go back to the data or field situation and look for evidence to support, refute, or modify that hypothesis.

Returning to our example of managers, a researcher doing such a study might come up with a hypothesis like the following to help elicit process from the data. In order to maintain control under different working conditions, the controlling manager will have to vary or intensify his or her actions/interactions, otherwise that control might break down. The researcher would then interview and observe managers, who are controlling, under different situations to see if and how their actions varied or intensified. The hypothesis would then be accepted, modified, or discarded in accordance with the field evidence.

Process as the Analyst's Viewpoint

One last point before we move to the mechanics of finding process in data. Process is the **analyst's way of accounting for or explaining change**. Rarely will a researcher hear an interviewee or person being observed refer to process, as such. It is unlikely that you would hear something like: "In phase one, this happened, then because of such and such I moved into phase 2, then the process was halted due to these events, so that I was never able to move on to phase 3. . . ."

Rather, you are much more likely to encounter something like the following words spoken by a manager of an assembly line.

> When the employees start goofing off and productivity goes down and we don't get the products out on time, then I have to put my foot down and enforce tight controls until they come around. I do things like not letting anyone leave early, docking people if they show up late, cancelling vacations, and putting off reviews and raises. Later, when my employees show me that they can work hard and keep to a deadline, then I relax my control a bit and give them a little more leeway.

Analysis. Sensitive to the idea of process, an analyst seeing the above passage would immediately pick up on the notion of process, the change in management style in response to conditions. He or she would note that a shift to a more controlling approach is deemed necessary by the manager in order to get the work accomplished within a scheduled time period. However, when the workers are able to meet the deadline, then the manager can relax that control somewhat.

Mechanics of Process

Since it is a change in conditions that sets process into motion, to understand the mechanics of process revealed by analysis it is necessary to understand something about change. What is change? What forms does it take? How and where does one find it?

What Is Change?

Change is reflected by a happening, an event denoting a difference in something. In what? For us, as grounded theorists, it is a **change in conditions of sufficient degree that it brings**

about a corresponding change in action/interactional strategies, which are carried out to maintain, obtain, or achieve some desired end in relation to the phenomenon under study. The notion of changing conditions brings **time** and **movement** into analysis. For rather than freezing action/interaction in time and space, the analyst shows how action/interaction change, move, and respond to changes in conditions that inevitably occur with the passage of time. The time that elapses between each change in conditions and corresponding change in action/interaction, which make up one part of a sequence or series, may be a moment, a week, or longer. The duration of, or amount of time between, each part of a sequence is not as important as the conception of its passage or movement.

The Shape and Form of Change

Change, like any phenomenon, can take many forms. It can be planned or unplanned, be great or small, occur quickly or slowly. Change has properties and it is these properties that give it **form**, **shape**, and **character**. Some of its properties and the dimensional ranges over which the properties might vary are listed below.

The list is not all inclusive and as you begin to think about change, you might add others to the list.

Properties	*Dimensional Ranges*	
rate	fast →	slow
occurrence	planned →	unplanned
shape	orderly→	random
	progressive →	nonprogressive
direction	forward →	backward
	upward →	downward
scope	wide →	narrow
degree of impact	great →	small
ability to control	high →	low

Thus when you are looking for or notice change in your data, you might want to analyze it in terms of the above properties and others that you might think of. For example, was its impact great or small, did it occur rapidly or slowly and what difference did this make?

How and Where Does One Find
Change That Points to Process?

To understand how and where to find change, one must return to the paradigm, first discussed in Chapter 7, and examine where along in the paradigmatic chain a change in conditions can occur and what can happen as a result of that change.

(1) Change can occur in the *set of conditions* that leads to or causes the phenomenon under investigation. When this happens it can set off a chain reaction leading to a change in context, and a corresponding change in action/interaction for managing, controlling, or handling the phenomenon under that changed context.

As an example, let us return to the study of pregnant women with chronic conditions as previously discussed in Chapter 8. When the illness (a causal condition of risk) became unstable during the pregnancy course, then the degree of risks perceived to be associated with the pregnancy changed, thereby shifting a woman from a lower-risk to higher-risk context. Correspondingly, her actions/interactions changed with the change in risk perception.

(2) There may also be a change in any of the *intervening conditions* that influence action/interaction. This too can lead to the need for changing or modifying action, in order to contain the associated risks. For example, the more confidence that a chronically ill pregnant woman had in her physicians' abilities to contain the risks, the more willing she was to delegate responsibility for management to them, especially when the illness or pregnancy was perceived to be off course. However, when that confidence was lost, due to what was perceived as an error in medical judgment placing her and/or baby in jeopardy, then a woman took back, at least temporarily, the part of

responsibility for management that she had delegated to her physician.

(3) Then too, *consequences* of previous action/interaction in one sequence of events can feed either back to (a) **add new conditions,** or (b) **alter the interaction among already existing conditions.** This means that what might have been a consequence of action in one action/interactional sequence within a series can become a condition influencing related action/interaction taken in the next sequence or at a later date. This can readily be seen from a commonplace example. Say the phenomenon under study is "crisis handling." If one successfully handles a crisis, then one would expect that the experience gained from handling that first crisis will affect how one handles similar crises in the future.

Describing Process

There are different ways by which an analyst might handle process analytically. We have identified two basic ways. You may think of others. One way is to view it as progressive movement, reflected in phases or stages. This is the usual way. Another way is to view it as nonprogressive movement, that is as purposeful altercations or changes in action/interaction in response to changes in conditions, but movement that does not necessarily occur in stages or phases. An example of each will be presented below.

Process Conceptualized as Stages or Phases

In order to show change or movement over time, an analyst can conceptualize data as steps, phases, or stages. The movement may be forward, backward, upward, or downward. Handling process in this manner is particularly useful when one is engaged in studies that examine passages such as: development, socialization, transformation, social mobility, immigration, and historic events.

When handling process in this manner, the analyst would want to spell out the conditions and corresponding actions that move the process forward; identify turning points; and show how the outcome of reaching, or not reaching those turning points plays into the conditions affecting the next set of actions taken to move the process forward. Added to this description, the analyst would want to account for variation in movement through these stages and phases. That is, why it is that some persons, groups, and so forth, lag behind and some pass through the stages at an accelerated rate, while others move so far and then plateau. Or, why it is that for some persons or groups there is actually a reversal rather than forward progress, or a failure to begin at all.

A note of caution here. Even when the core category is given a gerund ending that implies process or movement (such as **"managing** an illness course" versus simply calling it "illness course," or **"keeping** the flow of work going" versus "work flow," or **"controlling** awareness of dying," versus "awareness of dying"), it must be treated like any central phenomenon and developed in terms of the paradigm.

An example. One of the phenomenon that came out of our study of the chronically ill was one we termed "coming back" (Corbin & Strauss, 1988, 1991). This was defined as the process of returning to a satisfactory way of life, within the physical and mental limitations imposed by having a disabling medical condition. By "satisfactory way of life" we mean that a person learns to (a) accept and live with that which cannot be changed; and (b) make the most out of what there is left.

For purposes of this example "coming back" is defined as the core category. Whereas, "come back" itself, was seen as the outcome or consequence that results from undergoing the process of coming back. The causal condition that led to a person having to undergo coming back in our particular study was the presence of a disabling physical or mental condition that imposed limitations in the ability to perform life tasks. Disability has general properties such as degree, duration, extent, and time in the person's life when these occur. These properties set perimeters around how much come back (or outcome of the process) is possible, that is, how far one can come back, how fast, and so forth. But these properties alone do not necessarily determine outcome because of all the potential intervening conditions that also can come into play to affect passage, such as nature of the rehabilitation program or the degree of motivation and support.

Coming back as the central phenomenon also has properties. One is speed, which can range from rapid to prolonged or extended. It also has the property of degree which can range over a dimensional range from partial to complete. A third property is it has a course, which can be conceptualized as ranging in stages from: (a) Discovery of Limitations; (b) Embarking Upon the Come Back Trail; (c) Finding New Pathways; (d) Scaling the Peaks; to (e) Validation.

The course denotes the stages through which one must progress in order to reach come back. The other two properties, speed and extent, interact to give shape to that course, and will vary in how far and how fast progress occurs. (As we said earlier, these partly are determined by nature of the disability and partly by a wide range of potentially intervening conditions, like degree of motivation.) Based on variation in rates and progress, four different groups (contexts) were identified. These were the rapid and complete course; the rapid and partial course; the extended but complete course; and the extended partial course. Further variations in these patterns were found to be (a) Transcendence (going beyond acceptance and living with disability to accomplish noteworthy physical and/or mental feats); and (b) Failure to Embark (retreating into disability).

Movement through the coming back process was accomplished by means of three different but related types of action. These were termed: (a) mending or getting better physically through performance of medical tasks; (b) limitations stretching or increasing performance ability through accomplishment for rehabilitative tasks; and (c) reknitting or incorporating disability into one's conceptions of self, through completion of social/psychological tasks. Within each stage of coming back, these types of work took on different forms, importance, and division of labor. For example, early in the process getting better physically may be of utmost importance, therefore the emphasis is on performance of medical tasks by the ill person and medical personnel. Later, when physically well, the emphasis might shift to completion of social/psychological tasks, though all three types of work can go on to varying degrees at any stage.

Many different intervening conditions come into play within each stage to either facilitate or constrain performance of the three types of work, thereby affecting how much and how fast or whether each person coming back reached his or her potential. When the conditions were not favorable, if progress was to take place, then affected persons and those around them had to find some way of managing the conditions. For example, if the lack of motivation hindered progress, then health personnel or family had to use interactional tactics to rekindle motivation. If they were unsuccessful, then progress was slowed down or even halted.

Potential intervening conditions found to be significant in our data were: (a) the aspects of self that were lost due to disability were considered to be biographically significant, and worth the effort needed to carry out the work of come back; (b) the presence of clear and realistic goals for potential performances, with agreement about when, where, and how the performances were to be carried out, (c) a mobilization of forces to put and keep the person on the come back trail; (d) a come back initiator—someone to put the process in motion; (e) a come back coordinator—someone who took responsibility for coordinating the efforts of the various parties involved, usually a social worker or spouse; (f) a tailored fit between the come back plan and the person coming back; (g) each member of the come back team (person, professionals, family) performed his or her part in the division of labor; (h) appropriate resources— technical, financial, manpower, and so forth; (i) an ability to be flexible, to compromise, use humor, and to be creative; and most of all (j) periodic indicators of success.

While it is neither feasible nor desirable to spell out all of the details of the above findings on come back in this chapter, what we have hoped to convey was the complexity of passage through stages/phases, and how all of the elements of the paradigm must come into play to explain passage and its variations. Next, we would like to give a brief example of how process can be described as nonprogressive movement. Our explanation is brief. To enhance understanding, we suggest you might examine the research monographs referred to in the description below.

Process Conceptualized as Nonprogressive Movement

Some phenomenon do not lend themselves to conceptualization as orderly progressive steps and phases, yet process is very much a part of them. An example is chronic illness and its management. Though a chronic illness course can be broken down into phases, a person doesn't necessarily move between them in orderly progressive fashion. In fact, the whole aim of managing a chronic illness is to keep it as stable as possible, and to slow down, prevent, or reverse its potential downward course. Keeping a chronic illness stable in the face of constantly changing living conditions requires constant adjustments (Corbin & Strauss, 1988). Making these constant adjustments (actions) in the face of changing living conditions brings process into the management.

Another example of conceptualizing process in a fluid nondevelopmental manner can be found in the book *The Social Organization of Medical Work* (Strauss et al., 1985). The core category is "Types of Work" and the research is concerned with how it is organized and articulated in hospitals. The authors show that the work for the most part is subject to highly variable and changeable conditions. Even established routines "standard operating procedures" are affected daily—even hourly—by unforeseen contingencies. So, the flow and texture of the work in hospitals can neither be accurately described nor adequately analyzed without thinking in terms of process.

Summary

Process is the linking of action/interactional sequences, as they evolve over time. Bringing process into analysis is an essential feature of a grounded theory analysis. To do so, the analyst must consciously look for signs in the data indicating a change in conditions, and trace out what corresponding changes in action/interaction that these bring. Once identified, there are two main ways that process can be conceptualized in grounded theory studies. One is to view it as stages and phases of a passage, along with an explanation of what makes that passage move forward, halt, or take a downward turn. Another way to conceptualize process is as nonprogressive movement; that is, as action/interaction that is flexible, in flux, responsive, changeable in response to changing conditions.

10

The Conditional Matrix

Definition of Terms

Transactional System: A system of analysis that examines action/ interaction in relationship to their conditions and consequences.

Interaction: People doing things together or with respect to one another—and the accompanying action, talk, and thought processes.

Conditional Matrix: An analytic aid, a diagram, useful for considering the wide range of conditions and consequences related to the phenomenon under study. The matrix enables the analyst to both distinguish and link levels of conditions and consequences.

Conditional Path: The tracking of an event, incident, or happening from action/interaction through the various conditional and consequential levels, and vice versa, in order to directly link them to a phenomenon.

Our discussion in this chapter is a complex one but having learned the techniques described in earlier chapters you should be able to follow our discussion. What we do here, essentially, is to provide you with a **framework** that summarizes and integrates all we have presented previously, while at the same time explicates how the various kinds of conditions (causal, contextual, intervening) and consequences, spoken of first in Chapter 7, can be tightly woven into one's analysis. This is accomplished by purposefully and directly linking them to action/interaction. Actually, we've been speaking about this all along, especially in Chapters 7, 8, and 9. But here we want to make the linkage very explicit and tie our method of analysis together to form an explanatory framework.

After reading this chapter you may decide that you are not yet ready to master the subtle techniques we discuss. Perhaps, if this is your first or even second grounded theory study, you may not be prepared to undertake this final integrating step. But as you work with data and become more proficient in the method, you will see how the analysis all comes together.

It is the integrating detail, procedures, and operational logic for achieving this that **are the hallmarks of grounded theory** studies and that distinguish it from less tightly integrated and less sophisticated qualitative methods. So, we urge you to take up the challenge (when you are ready, of course) of aiming for the highest level of analysis that is possible with this method. The outcomes of your analysis, we assure you, will make your efforts worthwhile.

Grounded Theory as a Transactional System

We like to think of grounded theory as a *transactional system,* a method of analysis that allows one to examine the interactive nature of events. Of all the paradigm features, action and/or interaction lie at the heart of grounded theory. The manner in which any phenomenon is expressed is through purposeful and related action/interactional sequences. This is so whether the phenomenon is represented by a concept as abstract as "professional dominance," or as concrete as "illness management." All phenomena and their related action/interaction are embedded in sets of conditions. Action/interaction also lead to specifiable consequences. These, in turn, may become part of the relevant conditions that bear upon the next action/interactional sequence.

Properties of a Transactional System

A transactional system possesses certain properties:

(1) It is made up of interactive and interrelated *levels of conditions*. These range in scope from the broadest, or most general features of the world at large, to the more specific—those closest to the phenomenon under investigation.

(2) Conditions at any level may pertain to a phenomenon as (a) *cause* leading to that particular phenomenon, or (b) as *context* within which action/interaction take place, or (c) as *intervening* conditions standing between context and action/interaction that act to facilitate or constrain the latter. (These points were discussed more fully in Chapter 7.)

(3) Central to the transactional system, and located within the range of conditions, is *action/interaction*.

(4) Action/interaction take place in related sequences, thus are *processual* in nature.

(5) Various *consequences* arise out of action/interaction. These later may impact significantly on conditions at different levels. Thus consequences in turn may in some instances become significant conditions affecting the next action/interactional sequence.

(6) *Temporality* is built into the conditions. However, when we analytically stop the action/interaction to examine them, we view them cross-sectionally. We see them artificially, so to speak, as a slice of time, rather than over time, with relevant

pasts, presents, and futures. This point was explored in Chapter 9, when we discussed process and its importance in analysis.

(7) *Conditions* facilitate or hinder action/interaction. *Contingencies* that change conditions pose problematic and unanticipated situations and these must be handled.

(8) We refer to the transactional system of which we speak here as a *Conditional Matrix*. The latter term denotes a complex web of interrelated conditions, action/interaction, and consequences that pertains to a given phenomenon.

Merits of Using the Matrix

Before we discuss the details of this analytic tool, here is a listing of what it does:

(1) It helps you to be **theoretically sensitive to the range of conditions** that might bear upon the phenomenon under study.
(2) It enables you to be theoretically sensitive to the **range of potential consequences** that results from action/interaction.
(3) It assists you to **systematically relate conditions, actions/interaction, and consequences to a phenomenon**.

The Conditional Matrix

The conditional matrix may be represented as a set of circles, one inside the other, each (level) corresponding to different aspects of the world around us. In the outer rings stand those conditional features *most distant* to action/interaction; while the inner rings pertain to those conditional features bearing *most closely* upon an action/interaction sequence.

Conditions at all levels have relevance to any study. Even when studying a phenomenon that is clearly located at the inner part of the matrix—the action/interaction level—the broader levels of conditions will still be relevant. For example, participants in any interaction bring with them attitudes and values of their national and regional cultures, as well as their past experiences.

To maximize the generalizability of the matrix as an analytic tool, each level is presented in its most abstract form. **The researcher needs to fill in the specific conditional features for each level that pertain to the chosen area of investigation.** Items to be included would thus depend upon the type and scope of phenomenon under investigation. Specification of conditions may come from the research itself. Or they may come from the literature and experience: Then they would be considered provisional until data indicate their relationship to the phenomenon.

As we have noted, each condition within the matrix possesses the properties of time (through temporality) and place (location within the matrix). Also, one can study any phenomenon at any level of the matrix. For example, one might study world hunger, or hunger within a community, or organizational decision making, negotiations between countries, chronic illness in individuals, AIDS as a national problem, professionalism among nurses (a group), and relationships between arenas of debate within a community. **A point always important to remember is this**: Regardless of the level within which a phenomenon is located, that phenomenon will stand in conditional relationship to levels above and below it, as well as within the level itself.

General Features of the Matrix Levels

The outermost level may be thought of as the **international level**. It includes such items as: international politics, governmental regulations, culture, values, philosophies, economics, history, and international problems and issues like environment.

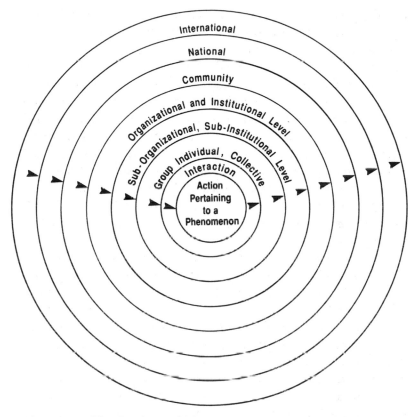

Figure 10.1. The Conditional Matrix

The second level may be regarded as the **national** level. Its features include national politics, governmental regulations, culture, history, values, economics, problems, and issues.

Next, comes the **community** level, including all of the above items but as they pertain to the community. Each community has its own demographic features that give it singularity.

Moving inward, we find the **organizational** and **institutional** levels. Each will have its own structure, rules, problems, histories.

Still another circle represents the **suborganizational, subinstitutional** level. This would include the peculiar features of a part of the city, hospital ward, or sublocation within a larger location, where the study is taking place.

Then, we reach the **collective, group,** and **individual level.** This level includes biographies, philosophies, knowledge, and experiences of persons and families, as well as those of various groups (special interest, professional, and scientific).

Later, we come to the **interactional** level. By interaction we mean people doing things together or with respect to one another in regards to a phenomenon (Becker, 1986)—and the action, talk, and thought processes that accompany the doing of those things. Even things done alone, like managing an illness, require interaction in the form of self-reflection, and contact with others to obtain medical supplies, counsel, and sometimes support. Interaction is carried out through such **interactional processes** as: negotiation, domination, teaching, discussion, debate, and self-reflection.

Finally, reaching the center of the matrix, we find **action:** both strategic and routine. This level represents the active, expressive, performance form of self and/or other interaction carried out to manage, respond to, and so forth, a phenomenon. Action is carried out through **action processes.** *These combine with interactional processes to complete the picture of action/interaction.* For example, the term "division of labor," which refers to an action process for the carrying out of the phenomenon of work, involves much more than different people doing different tasks to some end (Strauss, 1985). This process also encompasses the negotiations, discussions, legitimation of boundaries, and so forth, that take place in order to arrive at and maintain a division of labor and accomplish its associated tasks.

Examples of the Matrix at Work

We will now show how the conditional matrix opens up your analysis to a wide range of possible conditions that bear upon a given phenomenon, and how the matrix enables you to relate this phenomenon specifically to those conditions. The example is taken from a book on negotiations (Strauss, 1978). In it, the researcher states (pp. 77-103) that most writings on negotiations fail to detail the structural conditions under which negotiations occur; or if these conditions are discussed, they are brought into the picture only as a descriptive background. Thus what is missing in these writings is specific linkage of broad conditions to action/interaction.

To remedy this analytic problem, the use of a "negotiations paradigm" is suggested by Strauss. This paradigm provides a means of directly relating all of the various levels of conditions to negotiative interaction. Strauss breaks his conditions down into two basic types of conditional contexts: the structural context and the negotiation context.

The structural context refers to the conditions within which negotiations in the largest sense take place. These conditions represent the outermost rings of the matrix. In each case of negotiations studied, these conditions will be different. For instance, when studying the covert negotiations engaged in by corrupt judges, it would include such features as the American judiciary system and American marketplaces. In contrast, a study of negotiations between organizations would locate them within a context of national and international competition, governmental regulations, and so forth (see also Strauss, 1982, pp. 350-367).

The negotiation context represents the inner levels of the matrix. These conditional items pertain specifically to the phenomenon of association at the action/interaction level, and include:

(1) The number of negotiators and their experience at negotiating.
(2) The characteristics of the negotiations themselves; for example, whether they occur only once or repeatedly, or all at once, or in several phases.
(3) The balance of power displayed by the respective parties.
(4) Their respective stakes.
(5) The number and complexities of the issues involved in the negotiations.

(6) The clarity and boundaries of the issues involved in the negotiations.

(7) The alternative options of action as perceived by the negotiators.

By combining the two contexts (structural and negotiation), the analyst can more completely explain why any set of negotiations takes the form that they do. He or she can specify the nature of any set of negotiations, and the particular conditions that gave rise to them, including how outcomes of past negotiations come to bear on the present; also how the results of present negotiations will bear on future ones, by feeding back through the conditional levels and altering the levels. In treating conditions and consequences in this way, Strauss is integrating in a more sophisticated manner the causal, contextual, and intervening conditions we spoke of earlier. They are all there only not separated out as such.

Tracing Conditional Paths

The Conditional Matrix is operationalized by tracing *conditional paths*. Tracing paths involves tracking an event or incident from the level of action/interaction through the various conditional levels, or vice versa, to determine how they relate. This is done in order to directly link conditions and consequences with action/interaction.

Why Tracing Conditional Paths Is Important

Often, the presentation of a study begins or ends with descriptive lists of conditions that pertain to the phenomenon under investigation. That is, the author locates a phenomenon in a set of historical circumstances and events, or explains what conditions in a general sense relate to the phenomenon. This description gives us a background for understanding something about the context in which the given phenomenon is located or why it occurs. Yet, often, we are left only with this very general image, for no attempt was made to connect the specific conditions to the phenomenon in question, through their effect on action/interaction. Nor does the author systematically relate consequences back to the next action/interactional sequence.

The purpose of grounded theory methodology is to develop theory and not to merely describe phenomenon. And, in order for it to be theory, concepts must be systematically related, because it is *not* enough simply to say certain conditions exist and then require readers to figure out what the relationships to the phenomena might be. For example, it is not uncommon to read something like the following: "Technology has depersonalized medical care." However, unless one can show specifically how, when, where, with what consequences, technology (and which technology) has depersonalized medical care, and the strategies used to counteract depersonalization—then such a statement is so vague as to be meaningless. Everyone knows that technology can be depersonalizing, but what does depersonalizing mean in terms of what you might be studying? To put this in analytic terms: Conditions have to be given specificity by identifying them as causal, contextual, or intervening, in order to give them meaning in terms of what is being studied. The final sophisticated format with which they are interwoven into the theory is left to the researcher. In the discussion of negotiation we have provided you with only one way this can be done.

Tracing *conditional paths* also helps to put parameters around a study. One could easily become sidetracked, pursuing conditions that have no real relevance to the study. **By systematically tracing a path from action/interaction through conditional levels and vice versa, the irrelevant is less likely to be pursued.** You should only go after that which is pertinent because of its direct effect upon a phenomenon through action/interaction.

When analyzing data, you must either see the effect of conditions on phenomenon through action/interaction and their consequences, or you must deduce that effect from the literature or your experience, **but then find evidence of it**. Whatever does not show up significantly in the data is held in abeyance until it does or does not manifest itself. To be relevant, a condition or consequence has to be given meaning in terms of what you are studying. That is, it must be **verified** by data as having a **direct** or **indirect** effect upon the phenomenon.

How One Traces a Path

To trace a conditional path, you begin with an event, incident, or happening, then attempt to determine why this occurred, what conditions were operating, how the conditions manifest themselves, and with what consequences. You determine the answers to these questions by systematically following the effects of conditions through the matrix. What levels were passed through? With what effects?

This procedure of tracking conditional paths can be demonstrated through an example. One day while observing a head nurse at work on a medical unit, the researcher noted the following incident. A physician came onto the unit to make rounds, and while doing so she wished to check the colostomy of one of the patients. She asked the team leader, a nurse who was accompanying her on the rounds, for a pair of size six sterile gloves—a relatively small size. The team leader checked in the unit's storage area but the smallest available size was a seven. She offered these larger gloves to the physician, who refused them. This posed a problem for the team leader. Not knowing what to do, she turned to the head nurse. The latter explained to the physician that there were no size six gloves on the unit, suggesting the larger ones be used. Again, the physician refused. Now the head nurse was faced with the problem of locating the size six gloves. First, she called Central Supply, but was told that gloves of this size were temporarily in short supply, because of the large demand for gloves created by the AIDS epidemic. Therefore gloves were being closely monitored by a designated person, who presently was attending a meeting. The head nurse would have to wait to obtain the gloves until after this meeting. Meanwhile, the physician was getting very impatient. Consequently, the head nurse began to telephone other units, eventually locating a pair of size six gloves in the recovery room. She went to fetch them. The physician was finally able to proceed with the medical procedure. All of this interaction took about thirty minutes of the head nurse's valuable time.

Analyzing this incident, the researcher notes that work is **interrupted because a needed resource (in the form of a supply) is missing.** To keep the flow of work going, the head nurse will have to locate this resource: a pair of gloves. But the researcher is forced to ask: Why is finding these particular gloves so problematic? After all, gloves are not controlled substances, like drugs, to be kept under lock and key. What's happening to make this so, in this hospital, at this time? Following through with this question, the researcher—beginning with the interrupted action—traced the following conditional path. (The phenomenon under investigation was "work flow" as related to patient care at the organizational level.)

(a) We begin with **action,** which was interrupted because the needed resource was lacking. (b) Next, we move to the **interactional level** of the **conditional matrix.** The head nurse had attempted unsuccessfully to persuade the physician to accept the larger gloves. The physician had been adamant in her refusal. The head nurse then contacted central supply; here too she attempted to persuade, but was unsuccessful. Finally, she was able to persuade one of the other units to loan her some gloves. (c) Next we move to the **individual** level of the matrix. Another physician may have accepted the larger gloves, but this one refused. Her hands were small. So physical size plays some part in her refusal. (d) Then, we move to the **suborganizational** level of hospital ward, where the work occurs. Gloves were in short supply on the unit. Only a few limited sizes of sterile gloves were available. Why? Because they were being used so much. Why? Because of newly published national guidelines on infection control. To protect themselves and other patients, health workers were being asked by the National Center of Communicable Diseases to wear gloves when working on patients in a manner that might involve contact with their body fluids (since the patients might have AIDS or another communicable disease).

(e) Continuing on to the **organizational** level: We find that gloves are in short supply within the hospital. To ensure that each unit has an adequate supply for its respective type of work (surgery, recovery, etc.) gloves are kept under lock and key, and given only according to need. (f) Next we move to the **community level**, finding that the supply of sterile gloves here is also limited, for in this community many hospitals and nursing homes are following the same national guidelines. This brings us to production, distribution, and supply of sterile gloves within the community. Obviously, local suppliers were caught unprepared for the demand. (g) Now we move to the **national** level where the new guidelines originated, and ask "why"? Here we can trace the situation back to the current perception of an AIDS epidemic. So, we can show a relationship between AIDS and the work on a hospital unit by tracing upward through each of the conditional levels. Each level is more distantly removed from the problem at hand, yet in a wider sense contributes to it.

Following through on consequences in this illustration: We see that the work, both that of the nurse and the physician, was interrupted because of a needed resource. The physician did not complain, but might have done so, to the hospital administration about her loss of work time. Though the researcher did not pursue the matter further, it is reasonable to deduce that the increased demand for gloves, created by the national guidelines, did lead to pressure on the manufacturing companies at the community and national levels, and to an increase in their production and distribution of this resource, since several months later obtaining gloves did not seem to be a problem at the hospital.

Tracing conditions in this manner is quite different from saying that "AIDS is having an effect on hospital work," but leaving it to the reader to figure out how this effect actually occurred. Since we are studying how head nurses keep the flow of work going, we are interested in showing how the available resources (in the form of supplies) bear significantly on their abilities to maintain work flow. In this case, gloves were temporarily in short supply because of an increased demand, created by the national guidelines, which were proposed in response to the perception of an AIDS epidemic.

Now this illustration refers to a rather minor incident, and one whose conditional path is relatively easy to trace. Of course, a researcher would not want to trace every incident that was noted during a research project. One would choose only those incidents that seemed especially pertinent to the central phenomenon under investigation. Thus, in a study of work flow that was focused at the organizational level, a researcher might trace only those conditions and consequences pertaining to the repeated problems that were slowing down or interrupting work flow; or, conversely, those that were serving to keep the work flow smooth.

Studying Phenomena at Different Matrix Levels

In the following section we shall speak briefly and globally about how you might study a phenomenon embedded in **different** levels of the matrix. The main points to remember are these:

(1) All levels will apply but can only be brought into the analysis by showing their relevance to the phenomenon at focus. This can be done by tracing the conditional paths. The conditions and consequences will then be built into the analysis through the paradigm introduced in Chapter 7.

(2) Process must be brought into the analysis, in the form of changed action that occurred in response to changed conditions.

(3) Temporality in the form of past, present, and future is, in and of itself, a condition at each matrix level. Every interaction, organization, nation, and special interest group has a history. This history bears upon present action/interaction; while together, past and present become part of the future.

(4) There are also certain special features to remember. These are discussed below.

Interaction

When studying interaction, one would want to capture the evolving nature of the events, and what keeps the interaction going or what disrupts it. The first procedural step is to locate interaction in the immediate set of conditions that bear upon it, by asking: What is involved? What is its purpose? What form is it taking—that is, what are people doing, saying, thinking? What conditions move it along or stall or end it, and why? What transpires during the interaction? Are the interactants in alignment—that is, are they sensitive to the others; do their actions and words fit or is there misalignment, a lack of fit? What are the outcomes of each sequence, and how do outcomes of one sequence play into the next?

Then, you would also want to bring into your analysis of interaction the broader range of conditions. An important point to remember is that during an interactional sequence, interactants' responses are influenced not only by what transpires during the interaction itself, but also by what broader conditions bear upon the current situation. It is not enough simply to say that broader conditions (like social status or gender or beliefs and values) greatly influence interaction; you have to show how such conditions specifically influence responses and actions during the present interaction. In essence, you are placing the narrower interactional context within, and linking it to, this larger structural context.

Organizations

When studying a phenomenon related to the organizational level, any phenomenon under study would be located in the middle of the matrix, with conditions seen as bearing on it from above and below. Even when studying such abstract ideas as information flow or decision making in organizations, one would first want to locate them in action/interaction. This is because they represent the expressive forms that information, decisions, and so forth, take. For example, if one were studying decision making, one would want to know what decisions were taken, by whom, in response to what actions and interactions, and with what potential and actual consequences? One would also want to know something about the organization's past decision making, in terms of who, when, and with what outcomes. Then too, one must not forget the individuals within organizations who make the decisions, and whose careers and identities are often at stake in the decisions that they make. Also, one would want to determine the impact of still broader conditions on decision making, such as: economic and political considerations, national and international competition, federal and state regulations, and so forth. Unless consideration is given to at least some of these conditions, at each matrix level, an accurate picture of decision making at the organizational level cannot be obtained.

Biographical and Historical Processes

The conditional matrix is also relevant to the biographies of individuals, as well as to the histories of nations and organizations. Again, you would anchor the biographical and historical processes in action/interaction, both past and present. You would then show how conditions operating at a given time affected that action/interaction; along with the critical conditional junctures that facilitated or hindered their movement or change over time.

Substantive Versus Formal Theory

Levels and types of theory are sometimes confused. So, let us clarify the difference between those two matters here. One can have theory about a given phenomenon that is located at any matrix level: for instance, about an organizational or a biographical phenomenon. But the level or location within the matrix is not what characterizes a theory as more or less abstract (general). A theory about a phenomenon located at one of the outer levels of the matrix can still be a *substantive theory*. For example, if you were interested in "status," you could study the status of executives within an organization. In this case, the phenomenon is located at the organizational level of the matrix. Although midway between the broad and the narrow, it would still be a study of only one type of status situation: executives in an organization. Note that any substantive theory evolves from the study of a phenomenon situated in **one particular situational context**.

A formal theory, on the other hand, emerges from a study of a phenomenon examined under **many different types of situations**. For example, when developing a formal theory you might study status in several types of situations, say: the status of politicians at the national level, the status of persons within families, the status of socialites within a given city, and the status of various professional ranks within academic institutions. Note that even if you were to sample broadly—say, the status of executives of organizations chosen randomly from different parts of the country—you would still have a substantive theory. However, you could probably more safely generalize the findings about status to executives throughout the country than if you had studied executive status in only one organization, in only one region of the country.

The error sometimes made by researchers is that they think they can make the leap from substantive to formal theory because they have generalized to different types of situations from a phenomenon studied in only one situation. However cautiously a researcher may suggest the wider applicability of his or her substantive theory, this cannot be done with any assurance unless these other situations have also been studied. This is, indeed, how a substantive theory can be developed properly into a formal theory (Glaser, 1978, pp. 142-157; Glaser & Strauss, 1967; Strauss, 1987; pp. 240-248). In short, it is not the level of conditions that makes the difference between substantive and formal theories, but the variety of situations studied.

Summary

The conditional matrix presented in this chapter is a powerful analytic tool for capturing the many conditions and consequences bearing upon a given phenomenon. By tracing the conditional and consequential paths through the different matrix levels, one can determine which levels are relevant, and then relate them to the phenomenon through their impact upon action/interaction.

11

Theoretical Sampling

Definition of Terms

Theoretical Sampling: Is sampling on the basis of concepts that have proven theoretical relevance to the evolving theory.

Proven Theoretical Relevance: Indicates that concepts are deemed to be significant because they are repeatedly present or notably absent when comparing incident after incident, and are of sufficient importance to be given the status of categories.

Open Sampling: Is associated with open coding. Openness rather than specificity guides the sampling choices. Open sampling can be done purposively or systematically, or occur fortuitously. It includes on-site sampling.

Relational and Variational Sampling: Is associated with axial coding. Its aim is to maximize the finding of differences at the dimensional level. In can be done deliberately or systematically.

Discriminate Sampling: Is associated with selective coding. Its aim is to maximize opportunities for verifying the story line and relationships between categories and filling in poorly developed categories.

In this chapter, we will explore the meaning of *theoretical sampling*, a matter often confusing to people who do or read grounded theory studies. Questions that we address include: What is theoretical sampling? Why use theoretical sampling rather than some other form? How does one proceed? How does one keep the sampling systematic and consistent without rigidifying it? How much sampling must be done? At what times? How do you know when you have done enough? How does theoretical sampling differ from the more traditional forms of sampling?

Overview

Recollect that concepts are the basis of analysis in grounded theory research. All grounded theory procedures are aimed at identifying, developing, and relating concepts. To say that one samples theoretically, then, means sampling on the basis of concepts that have proven theoretical relevance to the evolving theory. The term **proven theoretical relevance** indicates that certain concepts are deemed significant because (1) they are **repeatedly present** or **notably absent** when comparing incident after incident, and (2) through the coding procedures they earn the **status of categories**. (See Chapter 1 for discussion of categories.) The aim of theoretical sampling is to sample events, incidents, and so forth, that are indicative of categories, their properties, and dimensions, so that you can develop and conceptually relate them.

Notice that we said we **sample incidents** and not persons per se! Our interest is in gathering data about what persons do or don't do in terms of action/interaction; the range of conditions that give rise to that action/interaction and its variations; how conditions change or stay the same over time and with what impact; also the consequences of either actual or failed action/interaction or of strategies never acted on.

Guiding the theoretical sampling are questions and comparisons that evolve during analysis and that help a researcher to discover and relate relevant categories, their properties, and dimensions. Asking questions and making comparisons serve different purposes in each of the three modes of sampling, as will be discussed below. Theoretical sampling will have different features depending upon the type of coding.

Theoretical sampling is **cumulative**. This is because concepts and their relationships also accumulate through the interplay of data collection and analysis. Moreover, sampling also increases in **depth of focus**. In the initial sampling, a researcher is interested in generating as many categories as possible, hence he or she gathers data on a wide range of pertinent areas. Later, the concentration is on development, density, and saturation of categories, here the data gathering is more focused on specific areas. **Consistency** is also important in sampling. Consistency here means gathering data systematically on each category.

Theoretical sampling ensures the noting of **variation** and **process**, as well as of **density**. By the same token, a certain degree of **flexibility** is also needed because the investigator must respond to and make the most out of data relevant situations that may arise while in the field. By flexibility, we mean the ability to move around and pursue areas of investigation that might not have been foreseen or planned, yet that appear to shed light upon or add a new perspective to one's area of investigation. Flexibility is also important when exploring new or unchartered areas because it allows the researcher to choose those avenues of sampling that bring about the greatest theoretical return.

For the most part, theoretical sampling must be well thought out: **planned** rather than haphazard, **while still retaining some degree of flexibility**. Rigidity in sampling hinders theory generation, which after all is the main goal of grounded theory. Sampling and analysis must occur in tandem, with analysis guiding the data collection. Otherwise, the researcher violates one of the most basic and fundamental canons of the grounded theory method: **sampling on the basis of the evolving theoretical relevance of concepts**.

General Considerations

In beginning a grounded theory study, there are many sampling matters that the researcher must think through. These initial decisions about sampling may change once the project is underway, yet they give the researcher some sense of direction and a place from which to begin. What happens once data collection actually begins is a matter of how well these initial sampling decisions fit the reality of the data.

(1) A site or group to study must be chosen. This, of course, is directed by your main research question. For example, if interested in studying decision making by executives, you must go to those places where executives are making decisions to see what they do, and obtain permission from appropriate sources to use that site.

(2) A decision must be made about the kinds of data to be used. Do you want to use observations, interviews, documents, audio or video tapes, or combinations of these? Here the choice is made on the basis of match—the method of data collection that best captures the kind(s) of information sought.

(3) If studying a developmental or evolving process, you might want to make some initial decisions about whether to follow the same persons over time, or different persons at varying points.

Initially, decisions regarding the number of sites and observations or interviews depend also upon access, available resources, research goals, plus your time and energy. Later, these decisions may be modified according to the evolving theory.

Interview and Observational Guides

When such initial decisions have been arrived at, the researcher is ready to develop a list of interview questions or areas for observation. (Usually, this must also be done to satisfy the requirements of Human Subjects Committees charged with protecting the rights of individuals.) The initial questions or areas for observation are based on concepts derived from literature or experience. Since these concepts, as you know, do not yet have proven theoretical relevance to the evolving theory, they must be considered provisional. Nevertheless, they provide a **beginning focus**, a place for the researcher to start.

Once data collection begins, the initial interview or observational guides should be just that: beginning guidelines only. To adhere rigidly to them throughout the research study will **foreclose** on the data possibilities inherent in the situation; **limit** the amount and type of data gathered; and **prevent** the researcher from achieving the density and variation of concepts so necessary for developing a grounded theory. **Remember, discovery is the aim of grounded theory, therefore data collection—and the associated theoretical sampling—must be structured to allow for this!**

Sampling Procedures

Sampling in grounded theory is directed by the logic and aim of the *three basic types of coding procedures*, as will be seen below. Furthermore, it is closely tied to *theoretical sensitivity* regardless of type of coding. The more sensitive you are to the theoretical relevance of certain concepts, the more likely are you to recognize indicators of them in the field and in the data. This sensitivity usually grows throughout the duration of a research project, and helps you to decide what concepts to look for, where you might find evidence of them, and how you can recognize them as indicators.

Since sensitivity usually increases with time, an interesting and important feature of grounded theory research is that **one can sample from previously collected data, as well as from data yet to be gathered.** It is not unusual in the early stages of a research project, for investigators to overlook or fail to pick up on the significance or meaning of certain events or episodes, because of a lack of theoretical sensitivity. Later, when developing new insights, an investigator can legitimately return to the old materials, and **recode them in light of additional knowledge.**

Sampling in Open Coding

The aim of open coding is of course to discover, name, and categorize phenomena; also to develop categories in terms of their properties and dimensions. **The aim of sampling here** is to uncover as many potentially relevant categories as possible, along with their properties and dimensions. As a result, sampling during this phase of the research project is also open. The sampling is open to those persons, places, situations that will provide the **greatest opportunity** to gather the **most relevant data** about the phenomenon under investigation.

In *open sampling*, selection of interviewees or observational sites is quite indiscriminate, in the sense that one could choose every third person who came through the door or could systematically proceed down a list of names. Since we are not yet sure which concepts are theoretically relevant, we may not know at this point the most opportune places, persons, or documents to go to for evidence of our concepts. At first, we are open to all possibilities and it is this **openness, rather than specificity, that guides initial sampling choices.**

During each interview, observation, and reading of documents, you want to absorb and uncover potentially relevant data. Therefore, it is best not to structure observations, interviews, or reading of documents too tightly. Rather, you want to allow sufficient space for other potentially relevant concepts to emerge; while at the same time thinking about conceptual areas that you have brought to the investigation or uncovered during the research process.

This open sampling requires considerable interviewing and observational skill, as well as a researcher who feels comfortable while waiting for something to happen or someone to say something interesting. This sampling also requires a researcher who knows how to probe without putting informants on the defensive—or worse, unconsciously signaling them to reply or to act in expected ways.

In open sampling it is crucial to maintain a balance between **consistency** (that is, systematically gathering relevant data about categories) and the **making of discoveries** (uncovering new categories, or new properties and dimensions).

Knowing how to **approach** subjects, how to **question**, how to **observe**, how to **read** documents or **view** video tapes: These are very important elements in the research process, and part of the researcher's characteristics that lead to and allow this important balance. Understandably, in order to carry out data collection through theoretical sampling, every researcher (whether a solo researcher or a member of a research team) *must* be skilled (and hopefully receive training) in interviewing and observational techniques, and sometimes in documentary research. Grounded theory research cannot be done satisfactorily using relatively unskilled interviewers (as is often done in survey research) or fieldworkers. If you need information about interviewing or field observational techniques, the following references should be of use: Burgess, 1982; Hammersley & Atkinson, 1983; Johnson, 1975; Schatzman & Strauss, 1973.

The process of open sampling. The initial data gathering is followed immediately by an analytic session in which you examine these data, according to the procedures discussed in Chapters 5 and 6.

As open coding proceeds, recollect that you make comparisons and ask questions about the data. These questions, and the conceptual products of comparisons that emerge (categories and subcategories), will then be added to your original list of questions and areas for observation. The succeeding interviews or observations are also followed by analysis as quickly as is feasible. Consequently, some concepts with which you entered the field will prove to be irrelevant, and therefore are discarded, modified, or replaced by those that arise during the research.

As for sampling: An important part of sampling here is making comparisons that give you the capacity to theoretically sample **on site**. While actually interviewing or observing, **you will be adjusting your interviewing and observing** so as to decide immediately on the focus, on what to ask, and where to look. Some questions or foci with which you entered the interview or observational site will quickly get dropped, or seem less salient, or at least get supplemented. This analytic sensitivity—amounting to theoretical sampling on site—that operates during an interview or observational period, will save time later. You won't need to reinterview or observe again in order to retrieve important missing data. Nevertheless, it is important to leave "doors open," so that you can return if necessary.

Some categories for which you are sampling will be arrived at inductively, as explained in Chapter 5. Others will come about as a result of deductive thinking during analysis. It is always important to remember each time to challenge the concepts and perspectives that you bring to the field; you challenge them against the reality of the situation, as you encounter and perceive this.

Variations in sampling techniques. Open sampling can be carried out in different ways. Since each has its advantages and disadvantages, a combination of all techniques is probably the most advantageous way to proceed.

(1) You may look, **purposefully**, for data bearing on categories, their properties, and dimensions. That is, you deliberately choose sites, persons, documents. For example, when doing a study on medical work in hospitals, one research team discovered that machinery in hospitals has several properties (Strauss et al., 1985). These included among others: cost, size, and status. The team then proceeded quite deliberately to sample events

and incidents related to machinery based on various dimensions of those and other properties, while comparing for similarities and differences. One type of machinery sampled was the CAT (computerized axial tomography) Scanner, because its specific dimensions (big, expensive, and of high status) maximized opportunities for discovering the differences made by such machinery to patient care and to the work of medical personnel.

(2) Another way to open sample is to proceed very **systematically**, going from one person or place to another on a list (or whoever walks through a door, or agrees to participate) looking for evidence of incidents, events, and so forth, that denote each category and make comparisons between these. Rather than maximizing opportunities to uncover similarities and differences, this procedure allows the researcher to uncover more subtle differences than might be evident, say, when comparing polar opposites. It does allow the maintenance of greater consistency in data gathering. We have used this procedure when studying the role of head nurses in keeping the flow of hospital work going. Since initially we knew little either about the particular hospitals visited or the head nurses, we simply proceeded from unit to unit, spending time with any head nurse who was willing to participate in the study. In the end, we found that each unit was different in terms of organizational structure, thus giving us a sound basis for comparisons of the nurses' work.

(3) Then too, data bearing upon open sampling sometimes, and even often, emerge quite **fortuitously**. You happen upon or find them unexpectedly during field observation, interviewing or documentary reading. It is important to recognize the analytic importance of an event or incident. This comes from having an open and questioning mind, and always being alert for significant data. When you see something new or different, you must stop and ask yourself: What is this? What can it mean?

Thus your theoretical sensitivity is linked during open coding with your theoretical sampling.

Sampling in Axial Coding:
Relational and Variational Sampling

Open coding is, of course, soon followed and paralleled by axial coding. Sampling still proceeds on the basis of theoretically relevant concepts (categories), but the focus changes. Recollect that in axial coding the aim is to relate more specifically the categories and subcategories that were uncovered during open sampling and coding, and to find evidence of variation and process with reference to them.

You relate categories in terms of the paradigm: conditions, context, action/interaction, and consequences. Thus sampling now focuses on **uncovering and validating those relationships**. You will propose statements of relationships; then while out in the field determine whether those relationships hold up.

Moreover, recollect that you want to uncover further instances of events and incidents that indicate differences and change in conditions, context, action/interaction, and consequences. You do this to uncover variation and process, as well as to densify the categories. This means that while out in the field you will want to **track** a category. **Again, questions and comparisons are important guides.** Is there evidence in this situation of this category's relevance? If so, what form or meaning does it take here? Is it the same or different from previous situations? What are its properties here? What conditions led up to it? What is the specific context? What intervening conditions have come into play to give this variation? What is the form of action/interaction? How do these change over time? What happens as a result? Your sampling now must bear on such questions.

The process of relational and variational sampling. In the relational and variational sampling done during axial coding, you try to **find as many differences as possible at the dimensional level in the data.** Here, as in open sampling, there are different ways that you can proceed. Again, you can do so very **systematically**, moving from situation to situation, gathering data on theoretically relevant categories. Another way is to **purposefully** choose persons, sites, or documents that maximize opportunities to elicit data regarding variations along dimensions of categories, and that demonstrate what happens when change occurs. However, the later procedure may prove difficult if you do not know a site, person, or document well enough in advance of the observation or interview to make that judgment. The procedure can also be difficult if you do not have unlimited access to sites, persons, or documents. Realistically, you may have to sample on the basis of those that you have access to or happen upon.

When you have the opportunity to choose who, what, and when to sample, then you may **proceed deductively** to hypotheses about relationships and the differences that might occur if you vary the dimensions of properties of a phenomenon. For instance, if the time of day seems to make a difference in a phenomenon of interest, then you might want deliberately to collect data at various times of the day in order more precisely to determine those differences.

The important thing to remember (again) in relational and variational sampling is this: The seeking of different sites, subjects, or documents is not the real issue. You have been concerned with **sampling on the basis of theoretically relevant concepts**. This is so whether you sample on the basis of what is available or are able deliberately to choose where to go for gathering data. When it comes to dealing with events and incidents, and the phenomena to which they pertain, rarely will you find any two or more events/incidents that are identical in all their conditional, contextual, action/interactional, and consequential relevancies. If sampling on the basis of theoretically relevant concepts, then you are engaged in theoretical sampling regardless of how the sampling proceeds. It may take longer to uncover process and variation, and to achieve density, when proceeding by **chance** (that which is available) rather than by **choice**. Yet this can be done, and successfully.

Highly selective (choice) sampling does become important however, when one is engaged in selective coding. Why this is important will be explained in the next section.

Sampling in Selective Coding: Discriminate Sampling

The aim of selective coding is to integrate the categories along the dimensional level to form a theory, validate the integrative statements of relationship, and fill in any categories that need further development. Thus sampling now must become very **directed and deliberate**, with conscious choices made about who and what to sample in order to obtain the needed data.

The process of discriminate sampling. In **discriminate sampling**, a researcher chooses the sites, persons, and documents that will maximize opportunities for verifying the story line, relationships between categories, and for filling in poorly developed categories. This may mean returning to old sites, documents, and persons, or going to new ones where one knows the necessary data can be gathered. For example, in the head nurse study, after completing data gathering in one hospital, the researchers planned to return to its various units to check out their theory. Furthermore, plans were made to gather data in other hospitals known to be organizationally different, in order to determine how well the theory held up there.

The importance of testing. **Testing** is a crucially important and integral part of grounded theory. **It is built into each step of the process.** Though not testing in a statistical sense, we are constantly comparing hypotheses against reality (the data), making modifications, then testing again. Only that which is repeatedly found to stand up against reality will be built into the theory. Recollect that negative cases are also very important. For to us, they denote not necessarily an error in our thinking but a **possible variation.** When a negative instance of action/interaction appears, it becomes very important to trace the line of conditions leading to it, in order to determine if this is failure or change in action/interaction. Was our original thinking wrong? Or does this negative instance indicate a variation, a new avenue of thought to be pursued? In all of this, as you can see, discriminate sampling plays an important role during the selective coding.

Theoretical saturation. At this point, you are probably wondering how long you must continue to sample. **The general rule** in grounded theory research is to **sample until theoretical saturation of each category is reached** (Glaser, 1978, pp. 124-126; Glaser & Strauss, 1967, pp. 61-62, 111-112). This means, until: (1) no new or relevant data seem to emerge regarding a category; (2) the category development is dense, insofar as all of the paradigm elements are accounted for, along with variation and process; (3) the relationships between categories are well established and validated. Theoretical saturation is of great importance. **Unless you strive for this saturation, your theory will be conceptually inadequate.**

Some Answers to Important Questions

(1) **Can I sample data from a library and how?** Some investigations require the study of documents, newspapers, or books as sources of data. Just how does one go about this? The answer is: You sample exactly as you do with interview or observational data, and then there is the usual interplay of coding and sampling.

If you are using a caché of archival material, this is the equivalent of a collection of interviews or fieldnotes (Glaser & Strauss, 1967, pp. 61-62, 111-112). However, the documentary data may not be located in one place but scattered throughout a single library, several libraries, agencies, or other organizations. Then you must reason, just as with other types of data, where the relevant events/incidents are to be found and sampled. Will they be in books about particular organizations, populations, or regions? You answer that question by locating the materials by using the usual bibliographic research techniques, including browsing purposely in the library stacks.

A special kind of document consists of the collected interviews or fieldnotes of another researcher. It is customary to call the analysis of such data by the term "secondary analysis" (Glaser, 1963). A grounded theorist can code these materials too, employing theoretical sampling in conjunction with the usual coding procedures.

(2) **How does one theoretically sample when on a team project and still maintain consistency?** When working with a team of researchers, as we said earlier, each member must attend the analytic sessions. Each must also receive copies of any memos that are written. Data must be brought back to the group and shared. The important point is that each knows the categories being investigated; so that each can systematically gather data on them during their own fieldwork. Equally important is that the team meets regularly and frequently for analyzing portions of its data. Working this way as an **analytic unit**, they all remain firmly within the same conceptual framework. Of course they also share in the making of major decisions about the theoretical sampling. As the data pile up, it becomes either impossible or not feasible for team members to read all of each other's interviews or fieldnotes, so of course each has the responsibility to code his or her own materials. Everyone **must read all the resulting memos**, otherwise the full resources of the team will not be brought to bear on the data nor analytic consistency be so easily obtained.

(3) **Can my theory be tested further by others?** Of course the theory can be tested beyond the testing already accomplished in your study. (See the earlier discussion about testing; also the discussion in Chapter 14.) Though one normally doesn't explicate propositions when writing about a particular grounded theory (they are built into the discussion), the hypothesized and systematically validated relationships between major categories are exactly that: propositions. These can be explicated and tested further, and separately if desired.

It is important to remember when doing so, however, that the conditions under which a phenomenon is said to exist are spelled out (or should be spelled out) in the theory. If you or someone else is to test a given proposition under different conditions, then it may well have to be modified to fit those conditions. Remember, a theory is just that—a theory. To find out through further testing that a proposition does not hold up, does not necessarily indicate the theory is wrong; but that its propositions have to be altered or expanded to encompass additional and specifically different conditions.

(4) **How does sampling in grounded theory studies differ from more traditional forms of sampling?** In quantitative forms of research, sampling is based on selecting a portion of a population to represent the entire population to which one wants to generalize. Thus the overriding consideration is representativeness of that sample, or how much it resembles that population in terms of specified characteristics. In reality, one can never be certain that a sample is completely representative. In quantitative research, however, certain procedures such as randomization and statistical measures help to minimize or control for that problem.

In grounded theory these issues are also handled and accounted for, but differently. Our concern is with *representativeness of concepts* in their varying forms. In each instance of data collection, we look for evidence of its significant presence or absence, and ask why? Why it is there, why is it not there, and what form does it take? Since we are looking for events and incidents that are indicative of phenomena and not counting individuals or sites per se, then each observation, interview, or document may refer to multiple examples of these events. For instance, while following a head nurse around over the course of a day, the researcher may note ten examples of her uses of power and her influence.

Naturally, the more interviews, observations, and documents obtained, then the more evidence will accumulate, the more variations will be found, and the greater density will be achieved. Thus there will be wider applicability of the theory, because more and different sets of conditions affecting phenomena are uncovered. If numbers are important for satisfying a committee or oneself, then instances of occurrence of phenomena can certainly be counted.

In terms of making generalizations to a larger population, **we are not attempting to generalize as such but to specify.** We specify the conditions under which our phenomena exist, the action/interaction that pertains to them, and the associated outcomes or consequences. This means that our theoretical formulation applies to these situations or circumstances but **to no others.** When conditions change, then the theoretical formulation will have to change to meet those new conditions. The purpose of a grounded theory must always be kept uppermost in mind. It can't be judged by using the usual criteria, nor can sampling be guided by logic of other types of research because its purposes, logic, canons, and procedures are quite different than in quantitative research. (See Chapter 14 for further discussion.)

In this regard, we note that one typical criticism made of qualitative investigations by quantitative researchers is wrong because application of their quantitative-research norms is inappropriate here. Their criticism is that qualitative data collection yields data that is noncomparable, because not all subjects are asked exactly the same interview questions. Whether it be interviews, field observations, or documents that constitute the data, the data are comparable because they are sampled by *representativeness of concepts.*

(5) **Can I combine quantitative and qualitative methods in the same study?** Yes you can, but be very clear about the purpose of those quantitative measures. They must also be built into the theory as further verification of conditions, action/ interaction, consequences, and so forth. In other words, unless the quantified findings are integrated into the theory, made part of the theory itself through the paradigm, they will be merely an aside.

One common error is for researchers to report they have done a grounded theory study when actually they have combined

methods inappropriately. They collect a little data, come up
with a few categories and properties, develop some general
statements of relationships about them, then attempt to validate their propositions through a survey or a standardized
instrument. Certainly this combination is appropriate in terms
of research in general, but this does not constitute a grounded
theory study. To meet the criteria for producing one, a researcher must utilize its general procedures and many of the
specific ones. Once this has been done, then the resulting propositions can be tested. This enterprise probably will take many
months, since by the end the propositions are (or should be)
very complex. (For a further discussion of criteria for judging a
grounded theory, see Chapter 14.)

(6) **When is the theoretical sampling complete? How long
do you have to continue?** You won't actually begin writing a
thesis, monograph, or book until most of your selective coding,
discriminate sampling, and integrating have taken place. Nevertheless, discriminate sampling often continues right into the
writing stage. Then it functions in the service of "filling-in,"
exactly as previously described. As a result of this sampling,
you may even find yourself reexamining the data and perhaps
even collecting a little additional data—but around very specific conceptual details that need to be checked out or filled in.

(7) **Is theoretical sampling difficult to learn?** It is relatively
easy to understand the procedural logic of theoretical sampling.
However, just like other grounded theory procedures, the sampling must be practiced assiduously, especially in actual research investigations, to make them "second nature."

(8) **What about research design, what is its relationship to
theoretical sampling?** Unlike the sampling done in quantitative investigations, theoretical sampling cannot be planned
before embarking on a grounded theory study. The specific
sampling decisions evolve during the research process itself.
Of course, beforehand you can reason that the phenomena in
which you are initially interested are likely to be evidenced at
certain sites, in certain organizations, and populations. When
acted on, these considerations can be viewed as a kind of

"research design." Realistically speaking, researchers when presenting proposals need to meet the expectations of funding agencies, and usually too those of subject-consent committees. An honest as well as the reasonable way of meeting these expectations is to detail carefully the provisional nature of your initial sampling rationale and procedures. Examples of sampling taken from your preliminary research should always accompany this discussion.

Summary

In grounded theory one samples events and incidents that are indicative of theoretically relevant concepts. Persons, sites, and documents simply provide the means to obtain those data. Sampling procedures differ according to the type of coding in which one is engaged. In open coding, one engages in open sampling; during axial coding, one does relational and variational coding; while in selective coding, one conducts discriminate coding. Sampling continues until theoretical saturation of categories is achieved.

Part III

Adjunctive Procedures

We have now reached the final part of this book. The third part is relatively easy reading compared with the chapters you have just completed, though very important to your overall theory development. Memos and diagrams are essential, for without these the researcher would have no written record of his or her analysis. There is no way that one can keep the results of such complicated procedures entirely in one's head. It is also relevant to know how to write and present studies once they are completed. Research findings are meaningless unless they are put into a form that allows others to think about, critique, and use. Finally, one must know how to evaluate one's own and others' grounded theory studies, not only in terms of the validity and reliability of the findings, but also in terms of growth and development as researchers.

The language of the above paragraph is direct, straightforward, as if all the additional procedures to be discussed in the next chapters are just to be learned and then quickly used. We need to remind you that neither life nor creative research are that simple. During the research process, it is not just insight and analysis that evolve—the researcher's cumulative experience also usually results in some changes in the researcher too. Down to the last steps in the writing, editing, and rewriting, you will be undergoing experiences: Some may be wonderful and exciting but others, alas, may be anxiety-provoking and full of struggle. The philosopher, John Dewey, writing about art, though he believed the same about science, expressed this eloquently and with a memorable metaphor:

> The act of expression that constitutes a work of art is a construction in time, not an instantaneous emission . . . [This] means that the expression of the self in and through a medium, constituting the work of art, is *itself* a prolonged interaction of something issuing from the self with objective conditions, a process in which both of them acquire a form and order they did not at first possess. Even the Almighty took seven days to create the heaven and the earth, and, if the record were complete, we should also learn that it was only at the end of that period that He was aware of just what He set out to do with the raw material of chaos that confronted him (John Dewey, *Art as Experience*, 1934, p. 65).

12

Memos and Diagrams
Definition of Terms

Memos: Written records of analysis related to the formulation of theory.

Code Notes: Memos containing the actual products of the three types of coding, such as, conceptual labels, paradigm features, and indications of process.

Theoretical Notes: Theoretically sensitizing and summarizing memos. These contain the products of inductive or deductive thinking about relevant and potentially relevant categories, their properties, dimensions, relationships, variations, processes, and conditional matrix.

Operational Notes: Memos containing directions to yourself and team members regarding sampling, questions, possible comparisons, leads to follow up on, and so forth.

Diagrams: Visual representations of relationships between concepts.

Logic Diagrams: Visual representations of analytic thinking that show the evolution of the logical relationships between categories and their subcategories, in terms of the paradigm features, as demonstrated in Chapter 7. A kind of logical, visual sorting process that helps you to identify how the categories are related to one another.

Integrative Diagrams: Visual representations of analytic thinking that are used to try out and show conceptual linkages; their format is not tied to the paradigm but left open to imagination.

When most people think of memos, they think of those written or typed forms of communication that pass between members of organizations (or families), which function as reminders or sources of information. But when we speak of memos and diagrams, we are referring to very specialized forms of written records: those that contain the products of our analysis. *Memos* represent the written forms of our abstract thinking about data. *Diagrams*, on the other hand, are the graphic representations or visual images of the relationships between concepts.

Memos and diagrams can take several forms: code notes, theoretical notes, operational notes, and subvarieties of these. In fact, a memo written at any one sitting may contain elements of one or more of any of these forms. It is important, however, to maintain distinctions among them; otherwise operational notes may become effectively buried under code notes, or lost in theoretical notes. The same holds true for diagrams. These can also take different forms, such as: logical or integrative.

Memos and diagrams evolve. They grow conceptually in complexity, density, clarity, and accuracy as the research and analysis progress. The later memos and diagrams may negate, amend, support, extend, and clarify earlier ones. It is truly amazing to see how our data base accumulates and grows theoretically, while maintaining its grounding in empirical reality.

Memoing and diagraming are important elements of analysis and should *never* be omitted, regardless of how pressed the analyst might be for time. **The memoing and diagraming begin at the inception of a research project and continue until the**

final writing. Memos and early diagrams are rarely published as such but, if sparse in number, the result will be highly visible in the finished research product: A theory whose concepts lack density and/or are only loosely related.

Memos and diagrams help you to gain analytical distance from materials. They assist your movement away from the data to abstract thinking, then in returning to the data to ground these abstractions in reality. Though much about memos and diagrams has been previously published, they are so important that their most salient features bear repeating and amplification here. (We recommend that you also consult Glaser, 1978, pp. 83-92, 116-127; Glaser & Strauss, 1967, pp. 108, 112; Schatzman & Strauss, 1973, pp. 94-107; Strauss, 1987, pp. 109-128, 170-182, 184-214.)

Some General and Specific Features About Memos and Diagrams

There are several general and specific features about memos and diagrams with which you should be familiar. We turn to these features next.

General Features

(1) Memos and diagrams vary in content and length by research phase, intent, and type of coding.

(2) In the beginning stages of analysis, memos and diagrams may appear awkward and simple. This is of no concern. Remember, no one but you will see your memos or early diagrams.

(3) Though you can write on your documents, this is poor practice, except perhaps in the earliest phases of open coding. We say this for several reasons. First, it is difficult to write memos of any length or to diagram next to the fieldnotes

because of the lack of space on the documents themselves. Second, some or all of the ideas and labels established in a given analytic session can be misleading and confusing when recoding a document at a future date (which usually happens as one's theoretical sensitivity grows). Third, it is difficult to retrieve information, in other words to combine or sort it, if the only place it has been written is in the margins. (There are several computer programs available to help the analyst sort and retrieve data. See Pfaffenberger (1988) and Tesch (1989) for further information regarding the use of computers in data analysis.)

(4) Each analyst must develop his or her own style for memoing and diagraming. Some may choose to use computer programs, others color coded cards, while still others prefer putting typewritten pages into binders, folders, or notebooks. The method you choose is not important, as long as it works for you. What is salient, however, is that your memos and diagrams remain orderly, progressive, systematic, and easily retrievable for sorting and cross-referencing.

(5) While memos and diagrams are crucially instrumental in assisting you to keep a record of the various development aspects of your theory, they also have other functions. Among the most important are that they free you to work with ideas using a kind of free association, one idea stimulating another without the constraints of either worrying about logic or staying too close to reality, **at least for the moment**. Later, of course, logic and grounding are important, but to be able to "see" what is in the data, you must be able to think creatively. Writing memos and doing diagrams help to stimulate this creativity.

(6) Another of their functions is to point out where the holes are in your thinking. Categories that are not fully developed in terms of the paradigm features, or whose relationships are not logical or firmly established, will quickly become evident when

you attempt to do a theoretical summarizing memo or make a logic diagram.

(7) Furthermore, memos and diagrams provide a "fund" (Glaser, 1978, p. 83) or storehouse of analytic ideas that can be sorted, ordered, and reordered, according to organizing scheme and need. These are useful when: You are ready to write on a topic; want to combine or cross-reference categories; or simply want to evaluate your progress—how far along you are with the analysis; also to suggest what needs further development and elaboration, or where further testing and validation are necessary. In research projects of long duration, it is easy to lose track of the status of the analysis. (See the further discussion of this at the end of this chapter.)

A few more general points. It is not necessary to code after every single analytic session. However, when stimulated by an idea, stop what you're doing and write it down, even if you don't write a lengthy memo at the time. Otherwise, very important thoughts can be lost. Later you can go back and elaborate, if necessary. Memos can also be written from other memos, as the writing or reading of one stimulates more thought about the same or another related idea. Or, you can write a summary memo that pulls together several memos. Or, you can make an integrative diagram incorporating the ideas of several smaller ones. Memos and diagrams can be derived from technical or theoretical literature as well as from real data. Any thoughts derived from the former, of course, must be considered provisional: to be confirmed later with actual data.

Specific Features

(1) Each memo and diagram **should be dated**. It **should also include** reference to the documents from which it was taken. The reference should include the code number of the interview, observation, document; the date on which the data was

collected; the page (and line number for those using computer programs); and any other means of identification that might prove useful in retrieving the data later.

(2) Each memo or diagram **should contain a heading** denoting the concept(s) or category(ies) to which it pertains. Memos or diagrams that combine or relate two or more categories or subcategories to a main category should **list all** these in the heading.

(3) **Short quotes or phrases** can be included in the memos. They are handy reminders of the data that gave rise to a particular concept or idea. Later, when writing, these can be used as illustrations.

(4) Memos and diagrams **should be broken down into their various forms** (see "Definitions" at beginning of the chapter) **and labeled** as such for easy reference. It is especially important to differentiate verified data from provisional data.

(5) When writing memos, one **should underline or italicize** references to categories or paradigmatic relationships for quick review.

(6) Any theoretical note that comes off of a code note **should make a reference back** to the code note that stimulated it.

(7) While an incident or event can pertain to two different categories, it is **advisable to code it under only one** to keep the categories separate and distinct. If in doubt, cross reference the item in another memo. Later as more data come in and categories become more refined and defined, the item can be placed under the appropriate label.

(8) **Don't be afraid to modify** memos and diagrams as the analysis progresses and new data leads to augmented insights. Memos and diagrams should reflect increased precision and

clarity in thought about categories and their relationships, as the study progresses.

(9) **Keep a list of emergent codes handy.** In the later stages of coding, refer to the list for possible categories or relationships you may have missed or failed to elaborate.

(10) If too many memos on different codes seem the same, **compare** codes or their dimensions for differences that are being missed between the two codes. If they are still the same, **collapse** the two into one code, perhaps under a higher order or more abstract concept.

(11) **Keep multiple copies** of your memos, for later organizing and sorting. Also if one copy is lost, then there is always a backup. This injunction holds especially true for computer copies, as anyone who has ever lost important data due to mechanical or user failure already knows.

(12) Indicate in your memos when you think a category is **saturated**, that is, thoroughly worked out in conceptual detail.

(13) **If you have two or more burning ideas** for a memo or diagram, jot each down lest you forget, then write a memo on or diagram for each to keep the ideas separate and clear.

(14) **Be flexible** and **stay relaxed** when memoing and diagraming. Rigid fixation on form or correctness stifles creativity and freezes thought.

(15) Finally—and this is the most important point of all—**stay conceptual in your memos**. They are not about people, or even about incidents or events as such, but *pertain to the concepts that represent abstractions of incidents, events, happenings.* As you know, it is concepts that move your analysis beyond description to theory.

Memos and Diagrams in the Three Types of Coding

For each type of coding, the memos and diagrams will look different, primarily because the purposes of the coding differ. Since analysis grows in density and complexity as the research progresses, so will the memos and diagrams.

How should memos look, then, at various points along the way? It's impossible within a book of this size and nature to give examples of each and every type of memo and diagram that could possibly be done at each stage of the research project. To do so would not only take too much space but also tend to rigidify the process. You have to develop your own style and techniques. However, in order to provide some guidelines, we will include some samples and give reference to previous texts on grounded theory where you can find illustrations of others.

Open Coding

Open coding is like beginning to work on a puzzle. You have to get organized; to sort out the pieces by color, which some-times includes noting minute differences in shading; so as later bit by bit to put the pieces together.

Those first pages of fieldnotes are puzzling. You don't know where to start, or even what exactly you're looking for, or whether you will recognize it if you see it. It's all an undiffer-entiated mass. All of this is reflected in your early memos. Here is the place to put down, without concern for what others will think and for what is "correct" or true, your first impressions, thoughts and directions to yourself. You can be as insecure as you want in these early stages. Just remind yourself, that if you or even others knew all the answers, there would be no reason to do this particular research.

Code notes. At first, your code notes might look quite sparse. During the first readings of your fieldnotes, you might read rapidly through and come up with a few conceptual labels, but with little sense of what they are really all about. With time, through the use of comparisons and the asking of questions, the code notes begin to take on some form. You might have a category and under it some properties and dimensions. Of course, the properties won't necessarily jump out at you from the data. Rather, it is more likely that you will come across a dimension of a property, then have to go back and ask to what property that dimension pertains.

Consider for example the following quotation: "The pain in my hands from my arthritis is really bad in damp cold weather. I wake up with it in the morning and it lasts throughout the day. The only time it seems to get better is at night when I am warm in bed and under the covers." We see here that arthritis has the property of pain, that's obvious. But the properties of that pain are not so clearly spelled out. They are given to us in their dimensional form rather than as general properties of pain per se. The analyst has to ask himself or herself: To what general properties do those dimensions point? What is the **dimensional location** of this **specific pain event**?

So what are those dimensions and what general properties do they indicate? First, there is the dimension of "really bad." One can conceptualize this dimension as pertaining to the property of **degree of intensity**. Pain can vary along a continuum of degree from very bad (severe) to not so bad (mild). Second, there is the dimension of **location in body**, the pain is in a hand but could be located anywhere in the body. Third, the pain lasts from morning throughout the day, which points to the property of **duration**. This can range along a continuum from long to short. There is also the property of **variation**: that is, the intensity of the pain varies. It varies with weather, time of day, and so forth. Finally, there is the degree of **continuity of the pain**. Is it continuous, intermittent, or temporary? In this case, one might say it is intermittent.

Your code note, therefore, might look like this:

10/7/89 Refer to fieldnote code #5, p. 6, dated 10/1/89
Code Note: PAIN AND ITS PROPERTIES AND DIMENSIONS (heading)

[Here you might put the quote that gave rise to the analysis.] Pain has certain properties, which then can vary along dimensional continua. Among these are:

General Properties	Possible Dimensions	
duration	long	short
degree of intensity	severe	mild
of variation	increases	decreases
location in body	head to	toe
degree of continuity	continuous	intermittent
		temporary.

[You might also indicate in your code notes where along the dimensional continua this particular event is located in terms of the dimensions. Thereby you describe this incident in terms of its specific properties—location along the dimensional continua. Here, too, you might want to designate the conditions that give rise to those particular properties (why they stand thus along the dimensional continuum). This begins to give you some of the specificity that you will need later, beginning in axial coding and more so when you integrate the categories in terms of their specific properties or dimensional location.] For example: Arthritis was the *cause* of pain in this pain event.

Under conditions of cold damp weather, the pain increases in intensity.

Under conditions of warmth, the pain decreases in intensity.

Under conditions of morning the pain begins. *Under conditions* of night the pain is relieved somewhat. Potential other category: *pain relief*. (Write another memo on this new category.)

This is an example of a simple code note. Notice that these conditional relationships are written as hypotheses, indicating that they are not accepted as proven, but that they are to be verified against other data to determine if they hold up and if they need modification. Notice also that we are in fact beginning the axial coding, which demonstrates how difficult it is in actual coding to separate the open from axial coding. With time you would continue to add to the list and elaborate on properties and dimensions of pain, specifying as much detail as you can or care to at this time. Taking off from this code note, you might come up with one or more theoretical notes.

Theoretical notes. Theoretical notes pick up where your code notes leave off. In a theoretical note you might ask yourself what are some of the other properties and their dimensions of pain and list them. Of course, these will be provisional and have to be validated with data. For instance in a theoretical note picking up from above, you might write something like this:

> 10/7/89 *Theoretical Note* written off of Code Note Pain Its Properties and Dimensions dated also 10/7/89.
> OTHER PROPERTIES AND DIMENSIONS OF PAIN
> Arthritis is certainly not the only cause of pain. One can also have pain from an injury, say a pulled muscle or a mild burn. Using my own experience with each of these, what else can I learn about pain? Well, pulled muscles or mild burns are usually the result of injuries, which make them temporary in nature rather than permanent. The property to which these dimensions point to might be conceptualized as **Pain Status**. How might I describe the pain of either? Pain from a pulled muscle is usually intensified when I try and move whatever body part is affected. This happens in arthritis also. This gives me another condition for intensification of pain. *Under conditions of movement,* pain due to a pulled muscle and arthritis is usually **intensified**. What about the mild burn. This is different. Pain of a burn can be described as burning in nature. Burning points to still another *property*, that is, **Type of Pain**. Pain varies in type from burning to throbbing, acute, or whatever. Another one of its properties is that pain has a **course** or **trajectory**. *Under conditions* of its inception, mild burn pain is more intense, *under conditions* of passing time, the pain diminishes. (And so forth.)

You might also write a theoretical note from an article that you have read about pain, or do an analysis of a research report about pain, or play some comparative games, or do a line-by-line analysis, or ask yourself questions about pain. This theoretical note is written to increase theoretical sensitivity and to give direction to further theoretical sampling. For instance:

10/7/89 *Theoretical Note* (Comes off of Code Note, 10/7/89, Pain Some Properties and Dimensions. Also theoretical note, same date).

QUESTIONS ABOUT PAIN

What are some of the *causes* of pain besides arthritis? There are many different causes of pain. For example, cancer, injury, surgery, tooth decay, amputation, childbirth.

How is pain *experienced* in each of these? Is it expected, not expected? Does being expected make a difference in how it is experienced? If it is expected, are steps taken to prevent or lessen it? If yes, how? What? If not, why not? What reasons would there be for *not* taking action to prevent or lessen it? Is some pain more intense than other pain? Does the intensity vary over time? Take childbirth or cancer for instance, is it more intense early or later in the course? Why? What is done about it?

How is pain *handled*? How does one convince someone that one is in pain? Do factors such as culture, age, how long the pain has been going on, intensity, and so forth, affect how one experiences and how one handles pain?

Operational notes. Theoretical notes often give direction for sampling, things to look for, seek out, ask about in the next interviews and observations. These are written then as operational notes. An example is provided below.

10/7/89 Operational Note

SAMPLING FOR PAIN

Based on my theoretical memo of the same date, it seems that I now have several different areas from which to gather data on pain. These will further elicit properties of pain, and give information about the different dimensions of those properties and the conditions that cause those properties to vary along dimensions. A good place to start is with childbirth. Another is to talk to persons with cancer. In talking to and observing these groups I should do so in terms of the properties and dimensions that I've already identified, and look for others that I might not have yet uncovered. For instance I will want to look at pain in terms of status, type, intensity, trajectory, duration, degree of, etc. I would also want to note the conditions that lead the properties to vary along the various dimensions. In other words, what conditions lead to pain being described as intense at one time, by one person, but not at another time or another person? Or, what causes type to vary, is it only the source of pain that causes this variation or do different people experience pain differently? Why is some pain continuous while other pain is intermittent?

There is virtually no limit to the variety of types of memos that might be written during open coding. You might write initial orienting memos; preliminary theoretical or directive ones; memos that open up thought on new phenomena; memos on new categories including their properties and dimensions; memos that distinguish between two or more categories; and memos that summarize where you've come from and where you're going.

The memos illustrated above exemplify types done during early phases of research and are rather simple, written to help the investigator get off the ground conceptually. Below is a more complicated theoretical note taken from a project on head nurses. It will give you an idea of what an open coding memo might look like somewhat later into a project. Note that it is still exploratory; that it opens up thoughts about two known *categories*, ideas to be explored in future observations. This memo is presented here exactly as written.

AS/JC 5/31/88 LOCAL KNOWLEDGE/ROUTINE WORK
LOCAL KNOWLEDGE IS SPECIFIC KNOWLEDGE
1. Specific knowledge that is *taken for granted* re past experiences with, for instance:
   instruments
   procedures
   practices
   places or spaces
   schedules, timing, pacing, etc.
   persons
   relationships: both work and sentimental
   moods and climates
   events

2. I think these items can be expressed in terms we have used before. We talked about *orders*. Thus there are: interactional order
technological order
spatial order
temporal order
sentimental order
(Maybe also institutional order—re organizational rules?) See how those correspond more or less to the above?

3. This specific knowledge is supplemented with, of course, *more general knowledge that's taken for granted.* That would include knowledge about days of the week, weekends, holidays, how hospitals work, medical-nursing knowledge of various topics, and more general cultural taken-for-granted knowledge.

4. When a new person is recruited to the staff, he or she either has to:

-be specifically taught the above local knowledge items in each type of *order* (where things are put, where to find this instrument, how we do this procedure here or indeed how to do this procedure that you don't know about yet, etc.).

-or has to pick it up himself or herself. The person can do this "on the job" re observing others or asking others during activity. Or can do this quite aside from usual activity, sitting them down and asking, even at coffee breaks. Or I guess can pick it up informally on the ward and off the ward talk.

5. But actually there is no possible way of teaching a new person *all* the local knowledge items. *Much of it has to be picked up during the work-activities.* AND THIS TAKES LOTS OF TIME. It takes even more time if no staff member cues the new person in or makes deliberate attempts to teach. Or if the person is unobservant, or too shy or lazy to ask.

6. IT'S IMPORTANT TO SEE that a considerable part of what we call *routine action rests on local knowledge.* One has only to watch people doing routine work to see that they don't have to even think about where to put things, when things have to be done unless the schedule's gone awry, how to behave when entering a room, etc. the head and body know what to do, so to speak, by themselves! In true John Dewey fashion, its when there's a problem—even a small one, that routines get at least somewhat mired down, that the staff person has to create something at least a bit

novel. Or draw on some past experience in handling that problem. The latter may also be part of local knowledge of the staff. Or it may be just her own. But note that in handling problems in new ways, local knowledge may be drawn upon as an ingredient in new action.

7. In time, as we have said before, a new way of acting may get institutionalized (either on the ward or at higher organizational levels). In that case, it becomes part of the specific-local knowledge on the ward.

Other examples of memos can be found in *Qualitative Analysis for Social Scientists* (Strauss, 1987, especially pp. 111-127.)

Diagrams. With early open coding, one has very little to diagram, for few relationships are yet established. Perhaps most useful at this time is what might be called a listing, rather than a diagram. In a listing for each category the analyst can delineate the properties along with the dimensions. This list could be extended as the analysis progresses. It provides the foundation that leads to the logic diagrams done during the axial coding.

Axial Coding

In axial coding we begin to fit the pieces of the puzzle together. Each piece (for instance, category and subcategory) has its exact location in the overall explanatory theory and must fit with the others to form an integrated whole. As when we build a puzzle, we pick up a piece and ask: Does this go here or there? Often our first attempts are trial and error. Later, as we become more theoretically sensitive, the fitting gets easier.

Memos. The purpose of axial coding, as you know, is to suggest and verify relationships between a category and its subcategories in terms of the paradigm, and to continue to look for variation in properties through their dimensions. Therefore, memos will reflect your successful and sometimes unsuccessful attempts to link the pieces together; your hunting for just the right connection. They will address questions like: What are the conditions bearing upon this phenomenon (causal, contextual, and intervening)? What are the strategic or routine actions/interactions taking place here? With what consequences? What happens when conditions change? Take note here again: As we said earlier in the book, the paradigm features and relationships don't carry color coded flags that wave at you from the pages of your fieldnotes. You have to search for those and recognize them for what they are. Sometimes this is difficult and so the early memos reflect your uncertainty, misconceptions, and feeble attempts. You must trust that with time the data will become clearer in their meanings, so that your memos will improve.

To give some conception of what an early code note in axial coding might look like, we give you the following example. First we will present an excerpt from a fieldnote, so that you might see the data we are working with. The phenomenon under investigation is pain and its management. It follows our operational note in the previous section directing us to look at pain due to causes other than disease. The pain being examined here is due to childbirth. Our interview was with a mother regarding her experience with pain during childbirth.

> You asked me to tell you about my experience with pain in childbirth. Its been quite a few years since I've had a baby. The funny thing about pain, whatever its source, is that once it's over, you kind of bury it deep in your subconscious somewhere. You can say that it was awful or not so bad, but this expression is filtered through a haze. You can't really feel it anywhere, you just have images of what you think it was like. Do you know what I mean?

> Childbirth is weird. You kind of dread it because you hear so much about the pain of labor, on the other hand you look forward to it because you're tired of carrying the child and anxious to see it. The pain is seen as the only way of getting there so you know you have to go through it. You just hope that it won't be too bad. Or that they will give you something if it is. The pain is expected, you think about it, dread it, prepare for it by going to classes and learning how to control and tolerate it. In the beginning it's not too bad, toward the end though, it kind of overwhelms you. The force just kind of takes you over. But you do have moments of rest

in between. And you know it is going to end, as soon as that baby comes out. And they can give you something to make it hurt less. I was lucky. I had short labors. So I didn't need any kind of medication. I just used my breathing and relaxing exercises. But I can see that if it goes on for hours and hours how you would get tired and need something.

10/10/89 Code Note
Analysis pertains to fieldnote Code #45, p. 2, dated 9/15/88.
PAIN, PAIN MANAGEMENT
CONDITIONS, ACTION/INTERACTION STRATEGIES, CONSEQUENCES FOR MANAGING THE PAIN OF CHILD-BIRTH

We are talking here about a particular *type* of pain event—that associated with childbirth. This association gives the pain experience its specific properties or location along the dimensional continua. The pain of childbirth is *expected* (degree of expectancy), can be *controlled* (degree of controllability) grows more *intense* as the labor progresses (degree of intensity also denotes that there is *phasing*), has a known beginning, onset of labor, and an end, delivery of the child (*course of trajectory*), and it is intermittent with periods of no pain in between (degree of *continuity*). Oddly enough, the pain of childbirth has another quality or characteristic that is quite strange and difficult to express. Pain is part of a labor process, labor of course serving an end—the end of pregnancy, the delivery of the awaited child. Hmm. How do I describe this property? The pain itself is not purposeful, but associated with a *purposeful activity*-labor. (**** I'll note this though I'm not yet sure what to do with this. It doesn't necessarily mean acceptance (though it might to some people), or tolerance, but perhaps it gives the pain a certain degree of predictability? This still doesn't quite capture this phenomenon.)

These specific properties of childbirth pain create the **context** in which the management of that pain takes place from the women's perspective.

From this fieldnote I can come up with the following *potential relationships*. Under *conditions*, where the pain (childbirth) is known beforehand, thus one can prepare; when it is intermittent rather than continuous; when its intensity varies over the course from mild at the beginning to more intense later; when labor is fairly short or at least follows a predictable course; and there are known techniques for controlling its intensity and these can be learned or negotiated for. Then, one can take action to control the intensity of the pain during labor through pain management techniques such as the use of relaxation and breathing techniques, pain medication, or anesthesia (caudal, pericervical). The *consequences* or outcomes of the use of these management techniques may not be absolute control but control of sufficient degree to get one through the labor.

One may enter labor with some *predefined* sense of what management techniques one is likely to use, such as breathing and relaxation techniques, however if the pain management context changes due to contingency such as labor becoming prolonged due to complications, then one may have to alter that predefined plan of management and use *supplements* or *alternatives* to those original techniques.

Other potential categories, properties to come out of this fieldnote to be explored in further memos are:

pain consciousness or memory—this seems acute at first but dulls with time. Phases of pain trajectory—this bears examining. Predictability of the pain and how this acts as a condition for management.

This fieldnote suggests but does not address: What about the timing and amount of medication, anesthesia? What are their effects, potential risks?

A *theoretical note* coming off of the above code note (related to but not directly off of the fieldnote) could go in many different directions. It might explore further the question(s) raised in the code note, suggest strategies for the management of the pain in childbirth, or pain due to other sources like surgery. It could look at other possible conditions that might affect the strategies that are chosen for pain management in childbirth and how they are carried out. It might examine consequences of the use of different strategies in terms of their ability to control the level of pain that is experienced. It might pull several memos together regarding pain and its management in a summary memo.

An *operational note* might also go in many different directions. It might suggest further sampling, or list hypotheses to be checked out in the next interviews. Or, it might remind us of the categories or subcategories we might especially want to focus on in the next analytic session.

For further examples of memos showing axial coding see the examples to follow.

Here is another instance of a memo taken from our study of head nurses that reflects axial coding. We were thinking analytically about the phenomenon of three work shifts in hospitals, where continuity of work must be maintained throughout twenty-four hours of the day.

AS/JC June 25, 1989 SUMMARY OF CODE NOTES ON THREE SHIFT ISSUES off fieldnotes June 20, 1989 Code #20 pp. 1-45 Notebook 31.

1. Conditions for EACH SHIFT

a. conditions as parameters, resources per work flow

b. conditions generative of contingencies

Therefore, routines (Organizational and ward and shift) plus strategies for handling these internal contingencies of shift, whether large or small contingencies.

2. Same for workflow BETWEEN shifts

Therefore routines plus strategies for handling between shifts (AM shift is central however).

3. Classic strategies for maximizing routines and minimizing contingencies information flow via a, b, c, d, n . . .

types of resources (manpower, supplies, technology, skill, time, energy, motivation) via a b c d n for each resource type

a) routine

b) prevention of foreseen contingencies

4. Routines and strategies however will also be specific to particular ward conditions.

5. Relative success or failure related to appropriate routines and strategies per ward context.

6. Note that routines (espec organiz derived) may precipitate contingencies. (Temporary or repeated—i.e. inappropriate)

7. So may the strategies.

8. The central role of the head nurse and her judgments, monitoring, assessing, negotiating, etc. SHE CONSTITUTES, IN OTHER WORDS, A SPECIAL SET OF STRUCTURAL CONDITIONS affecting the work on each shift.

Note: re the 3 shift issue: all of our concepts should work here also: i.e., local knowledge, routines, resources, power, climate, mood, ideology, d/l. etc.

Below is another memo taken from the same source. This is a *theoretical note*. Notice the hypotheses and how they are built into the memo.

AS/JC 7-22-88 (Telephone)
************IMPORTANT MEMO: ROUTINE/NOVEL

I posed the issue, long ago observed, that nurses encountered typical problems—often costly of time and effort and sentiment—but do *not act to change institutional rules or procedures to prevent. Rather they go on with their institutionalized-routine ways of doing work.* (Problematic dying patients for instance, or as in pain book). Rather they typify this patient as like one(s) they have had before. But afterward there is no institutional change. These I have thought for a long time are due to the way organizations get work done, their priorities, and perhaps structural strains that precipitate recurrent semicrises. But here is a much better and detailed set of answers.

1. *When work processes break down, then there is a change of procedure.*

2. *If they don't change procedures, it's because the work associated with the problem is not of high priority.* The nurses are SO BUSY doing the high priority work, that they don't have time and effort to do anything else. They will, in fact, if the problem (like a problem patient) gets bad enough call in specialists—social workers, chaplains, psychiatrists—because their own work has to go on. Or they will ignore the patient; perhaps making the problem worse, but.

3. *If the work affected by the breakdown of work process is of high priority (like affect its efficiency or patient's safety), then they have to reflect on how to prevent this from occurring again.*

a) *If the change is easily done*, then it is done through interactional processes: negotiation, persuasion, even some coersion.

b) *If the change will be difficult organizationally*, this essentially means a lot of additional work must be done—but it must be done—that is: figuring out what's to be done, planning decision making, persuading, negotiating, finding new resources, acting to raise motivation, additional supervising when the new routines are instituted, etc. And of course, an additional drain on the total articulation process until everything is acting smoothly again.

4. So, what we are saying is that THESE ARE THE *CONDITIONS FOR AND MECHANISMS THROUGH* WHICH ACTION IS INSTITUTED TO REPLACE ROUTINES WITH NEW INSTITUTIONALIZED PROCEDURES. *Notice*: we have to look more closely at the meaning of routine procedures. At the lowest level, it means how tasks are done. But this can be done by staff agreement as well as by administrative rules.

Diagrams. In axial coding, diagrams begin to take on form. Initial logic diagrams such as those shown in Chapter 7 can be useful for sorting out the various relationships. You might want to do integrative diagrams to help uncover potential relationships between a category and its subcategories or between several categories, like the two shown below. These early diagrams will be crude. They become more complex with time. (For examples of the changes that take place in integrative diagrams over time, see Strauss, 1987, pp. 174-178.)

Figures 12.1, 12.2, and 12.3 are examples of various types of diagrams that can be helpful in discovering relationships in data.

Selective Coding

Selective coding denotes the final step in our analysis: The integration of concepts around a core category and the filling in of categories that need further development and refinement. At this time, memos and diagrams show depth and complexity of thought that serve as mirrors of the evolving theory.

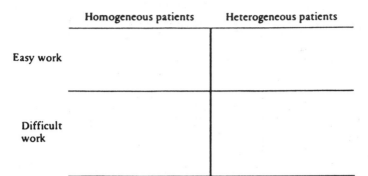

Figure 12.1. Homogeneous/Heterogeneous Patients × Easy/Difficult Work

Phase of illness	Number of machines Few–Many			Frequency Few-Intermittent-Often			Duration Short-Forever	
Early								
Middle								
Late								

Figure 12.2. Illness Course: Machine–Time Dimension

Code notes. In selective coding there tends to be fewer code notes, with the greatest concentration of efforts directed at theoretical notes. The code notes are likely to pertain mostly to the filling in of categories.

Theoretical notes. It is in the form of a theoretical note that we write the first descriptive rendition of what the research is all about. This theoretical memo will serve as a stepping-off point for the analytic story that is to follow. (For examples of what

Consequences For

Pain Tasks	Illness trajectory	Life and death	Carrying on	Interaction	Ward work	Sentimental order	Personal identity
Diagnosing							
Preventing							
Minimizing							
Inflicting							
Relieving							
Enduring							
Expressing							

Figure 12.3. A Balancing Matrix

is meant, review Chapter 8 in this book.) It is from these "story telling" memos that we come to identify the core category (central phenomenon) and to integrate other categories around it. We will also spell out these relationships as hypotheses in theoretical notes.

Operational notes. Operational notes in selective coding tend to be very specific. "Go here or there. Check out this or that? Do this, that." By now, we approach our work with confidence. We are no longer exploring, but using our time to validate our findings and refine our theory.

Diagrams

Diagrams in selective coding show the density and complexity of the theory. Often, because of this, it is difficult to translate the theory from words into a concise and precise graphic form. Yet, the very act of doing so will help you to classify and systematize the relationships that exist between categories and the core category. In the end, it is important to have this

220 BASICS OF QUALITATIVE RESEARCH

unencumbered graphic version of the theory available to aid others in visualizing and comprehending your theory as well as assist you to keep the relationships clear when writing. Figure 12.4 is an example of an integrative diagram, taken from our work on "trajectory." This diagram went through many revisions before the authors arrived at the final version.

Another point: Integrative diagrams can correspond to different parts of your theory. For example, you might have a diagram that deals specifically with one major category and all its subcategories as shown in Figure 12.5.

The Sorting of Memos and Diagrams

An image that comes to mind when we think of sorting is of an inexperienced grounded theorist standing with stacks of memos in his or her hands; then, dropping them one by one, letting them fall where they will. The piles that result represent a fortuitous sorting of the concepts. There are times when we all feel this way, especially in those darkest days when we're inundated with data and ideas but can't quite comprehend how they come together. We know there is order, but it seems beyond our comprehension; it seems like our theory could go this way or that.

Yet those of us with experience know that indeed there is order, and that our memos and diagrams hold the key to that order. By **reading and rereading** them, then by **sorting** them, we can begin to discover how the categories come together around a core category. From our general reading of the memos, we write a descriptive story. Then using the categories (analytic terms) in our memos, we translate our descriptive story into an analytic one. The logic and order are all there (or should be, if the procedures in this book were followed).

In practical terms, once we have some idea of how our categories come together, some organizing scheme (worked out through the writing of our descriptive and analytic stories and

TIME

REFLECTION PROCESS

Contextualizing

Looping Process

Crystallization
decrystallization
recrystallization

Trajectory with Biography —— Degrees of Contextualizing

segmented
integrated
?

reviews

Trajectory/Biography
recalls

interpreted in present

Time

projections

The BBC Chain

Conceptions of Self

Biography

Body

Coming to Terms - takes place through: confrontations

brought about by:
trajectory changes
biographical changes
interaction
activity/behavior

with:
chronicity
limitations
death

leads to integration/reintegration process - varies 0 to 100%

takes place through:
letting go
grieving
reconstructing

from/to:
nonacceptance
acceptance
transcendence

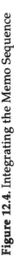

Figure 12.4. Integrating the Memo Sequence

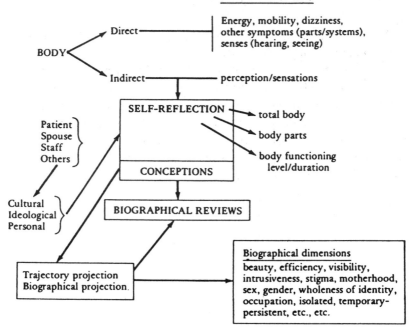

Figure 12.5. Body, Biography, Trajectory

integrative diagrams), we can then group our memos according to this scheme. **Sorting is important because it finalizes our integration**. With this finalization, we can then try out our scheme on some of our research subjects, on our colleagues, committee members, friends, spouses, and companions. This finalization enables us to write on each topic in detail, as well as on the integrated whole.

Sorting earlier serves another useful process. By looking back over memos and diagrams and grouping them, we can tell what we know about a topic and where further clarifying information is needed. This procedure gives us a kind of interim—not quite final—status report.

Summary

Memos and diagrams are essential procedures in the analysis, varying by the three types of coding. They enable the analyst to keep an ongoing record of the analytic process. Memos contain the products of actual coding, plus theoretically sensitizing and summarizing notes, and give direction for sampling. Diagrams are visual representations of the relationships between concepts. Both memos and diagrams will enter into the next step of your enterprise—writing for publication and giving talks about your research.

13

Writing Theses and Monographs, and Giving Talks About Your Research

Finally, there are those inevitable questions about writing for publication that are associated with every research project.

(1) When should I begin writing up the research for publication? How do I know when the research is ready for writing up?

(2) What shall I write about?

(3) What form(s) should the writing take—papers, a monograph, something else?

(4) Is writing papers different than writing monographs (or theses)?

(5) What about oral presentations?

(6) Should I try to publish? Where should I publish?

(7) What audiences am I writing for (including when I am writing a thesis)?

(8) What should the styles of writing look like?

(9) How do I get started on the actual writing, or the outline for it?

(10) How will I know when the writing is good enough to submit for publication?

In this chapter, we attempt to give useful answers to such questions. There will be three sections. The first is addressed to verbal presentations; the second to monographs and theses; the third to various types of papers. (The parallel readings to this chapter that you might consult are Glaser, 1978, pp. 128-141; Strauss, 1987, pp. 249-264.)

Introductory Remarks

From Analysis to Writing

Before you plunge into the next pages, we suggest rereading or at least scanning Chapter 8 on integration, and Chapter 12 on memos and diagrams. There you will be reminded that when you actually sit down to write about your research—or even outline a preliminary talk or paper—a great many aids to these presentations will already have been built into your work. The many months of prior effort put into analysis will now pay off. Among the analytic aids are your memos, operational and integrative diagrams, and the tracing of relationships among core and subcategories; but also there is your overall analytic story. It is on these materials that the presentations will be constructed. Yet the materials cannot be put between covers and published "as is." The problem is how to translate these analytic materials clearly and effectively so that others can benefit from them. Working on this translation will further clarify your analyses.

Why Publish?

A few more prefatory words should be said about a prior question: Why publish at all? Doctoral or masters' theses aside (as two species of semipublic nonpublications), if you do not publish then your analyses remain private, except perhaps for talking with friends and a few speeches made in public. There are a variety of reasons for publishing. One or more may lie behind the considerable effort it takes to get something written, edited, and approved of by editors of journals or publishing companies. Without reviewing the many motivations (such as self-pride, career advancement, desire to contribute to reform, or to illuminate the lives of people studied), there is the paramount obligation to communicate with colleagues. No research knowledge can accumulate, whether disciplinary or professional, nor can its implications for practice and theory be usefully developed, without the fulfillment of this obligation. Experienced researchers generally have this obligation built into their psyches. The less experienced, and especially graduate students doing "real" research for the first time, may not only lack motivation to publish but many undervalue their own research. If a researcher believes this and his or her sponsors or friends believe this also, then reluctance to go public may have a legitimate basis. If not, collegial obligation should be honored.

Verbal Presentations

Often researchers present materials orally as a trial run, to see how a given audience will react to these presentations. Indeed, sometimes those who are being studied will directly or indirectly press a researcher: "What are you finding?" "Can't you give us at least preliminary findings or interpretations?" Either in an attempt to satisfy their curiosities or to get feedback, or for other reasons, many investigators find it useful to make oral presentations. They even do this fairly early in their research projects. Grounded theory studies lend themselves to relatively early reporting, because the analyses begin at the outset of the projects. **It is not at all necessary to wait until a finer grained analysis is completed** to satisfy listeners: Whether they are just curious, avid for results, skeptical, or merely want to test the researcher.

Naturally you should try to guess, by virtue of your interviews or field observations, what subjects the listeners might be most interested in, and to what style of presentation they would be most responsive. Collegial audiences can absorb a greater amount of talk couched at more abstract levels, and even talks devoted to research strategies and experiences. Other audiences may respond well only to discussions of concepts and conceptual relationships if spiced with narrative or case materials, or with vivid examples, including actual quotations from the people interviewed. You also need to choose carefully the appropriate level of vocabulary for each audience if possible. A bad choice can turn off an audience, a good one can make all the difference in getting ideas across. If there is a discussion or question/answer period after the talk, then no matter how early or late in the life of your research project, this extra time can be turned into an informal collective interview that adds to your data. The audience also unwittingly functions to corroborate your theoretical formulations or prompt you to qualify them.

It should be obvious from the above sentences that a **conception of audience is very important** for a successful verbal presentation. No less important is that you really do have something to say to particular groups of listeners. If the analyses are grounded firmly in data, then the cards are further stacked in your favor. Also if the talk is to the "natives" themselves then a successful talk is additionally probable. If, on the other hand, your audience is a collegial one, then, of course, good theoretical or professional-practitioner sensitivity will improve your chances of having appreciative listeners.

All of this advice you may think is still rather general, although perhaps somewhat reassuring. What about the practical question of how one actually decides on the topic of a talk or speech? In grounded theory studies, given the considerable number of categories generated through coding, how in the world does anybody decide which ones to talk about in a speech? Also, what about all those associated conditions, strategies, and consequences, let alone the larger theoretical framework itself?

Keeping in mind that a talk's content should be matched as far as possible with audience, we suggest the following answers. To begin with, generally it is far better *not* to present the entire theoretical framework. This is just too much for most audiences to digest, even very theoretically literate ones. It also takes a great deal of skill to present the many categories and their relationships clearly enough so that listeners can both understand them and keep them in mind. You can, of course, sketch the main descriptive story and then translate a bit of it into an analytic story before turning to an elaboration of one of its more interesting features. However, we believe a verbal presentation will be more effective, and certainly better grasped and remembered, if it focuses on the discussion of **only one or two categories**.

For instance, say you have discovered that the work of hospitalized patients is virtually invisible to the nurses and physicians. This category of **patient work** can then be discussed in terms of why, when, and how it occurs—touching on various relevant conditions; also what consequences there are for the staff's work and the patients' care, reputations, and so on. The different subtypes of work that patients engage in can be sketched also. The different conditions under which this work is actually recognized by the personnel or not, appreciated or not, can also be discussed. The speaker might even end on a rhetorical note, varying the content by whether the listeners are health professionals ("you should know this in order to improve the care of patients") or laymen ("you should insist that this work is valuable and should be explicitly recognized as such by the professionals"). Focusing on one or two categories you can still weave in subsidiary ones, such as **comfort work** or **safety work** without muddying your talk.

Developing a presentation around one or two categories involves writing a clear outline of the main story with regard to them, and fitting in some subsidiary categories and relevant paradigm items. Even to a relatively unsophisticated audience, you should be able to present a clear and intriguing story. The totality of the grounded theory as constituted up to that moment remains in the background, but provides the invisible springboard from which the speech is constructed. On the other hand, the speech only offers a small slice of the entire analysis.

Writing Monographs or Theses

Resources and Impediments

When writing a monograph or thesis, you begin with special reliance on several instruments. The most important is *you*. Over the course of a research project you have gained an increased theoretical sensitivity to the many facets of the phenomena under study. You have also learned a great deal substantively about the phenomena. Both of these will come into play as you write, reminding you of data that is now "in your head" as well as where data can be refound if necessary in the field notes or interviews.

Of course, you have other skills too, implicit ones perhaps, that will further the writing: Some sense of how to construct sentences and put them together, without too many grammatical errors, and so on. Unfortunately you can also be, as the saying goes, your own worst enemy when it comes to writing. Aside from poor writing skills, you may have all the usual writers' blocks described in books designed to help people write (see Becker, 1986b).

Fortunately you have learned essential analytic procedures. These will help to get you into the first phases of writing. They also are used throughout all of its successive phases, and may even continue into your rewriting of final drafts of the manuscript. This writing requires:

(1) A clear analytic story
(2) Writing on a conceptual level, with description kept secondary
(3) The clear specification of relationships among categories, with levels of conceptualization also kept clear
(4) The specification of variations and their relevant conditions, consequences, and so forth, including the broader ones.

Since these requirements are so like the analytic procedures discussed in this book, you can see that good analyses should greatly help in the actual writing.

Procedures

When beginning to think of writing, you should review the last integrative diagrams and sort the memos until there is no question what is the main analytic story line that you wish to tell. This review is followed by enough further sorting of memos to give confidence that a reasonably good, although still provisional, outline can be written. The sorting might even raise some doubts that your analytic story was not altogether accurate. If so, don't be discouraged: The worst that should happen is that the analytic story becomes qualified, and so improved. At any rate, the story must be translated into an overall outline. Some people do not work well with detailed outlines. Yet, because of our own experiences and those of our students' we give the following advice: at least **sketch an overall logic outline**.

In this translation of analysis to an outline, there are additional procedures that can be of help. The first is to think intently about the **analytic logic** that informs the story. Every research monograph, indeed every research paper, will have such a logic. Each has a key sentence or paragraph that signals the author's underlying "little logic" (Glaser, 1978, pp. 129-130), though sometimes the authors seem not to be aware of this. This signal of what is central to any given publication (or thesis for that matter) is often found in the first paragraph or pages and then again in the closing page or pages. As for your own manuscript, even the first draft should have its essential analytic story presented clearly. In a sense the entire thesis or monograph will represent a spelling out of this analytic story.

A second procedure for translating analysis into writing is to **construct outlines**. An outline involves the provisional listing and ordering of chapters. Logic outlines, linking each section together and the placing of each in its prospective order, can be written later for each chapter, if that seems to aid your thinking—as generally it does. Chapter outlines are filled in and ordered by thinking about sections and subsections—always in relation to the entire chapter. Essential to these decisions is the **sorting** of whatever memos seem relevant. Even when you finally write a chapter and its component sections, you will find yourself **scanning** or **rereading** the pertinent memos.

In the preface or opening chapter of the manuscript, you should give a clear **summary statement** of the main outline. This statement as well as the outline itself can later be revised if deemed necessary. You can write the statement just as soon as you figure out the outline or soon after; but this can also be done after the first draft is finished when you have a better sense of what you have accomplished. "Some [people] prefer, from the beginning, to keep a tight rein on what they will write. It forces them to [stay close to their sorting]. Others do it last when reworking drafts" (Glaser, 1978, p. 132).

A third procedure involves **imagining visually the "architecture"** of your main outline. Visualizing this structure amounts to a kind of spatial metaphor. We can illustrate this by a story and three examples of such metaphors. A colleague once characterized two monographs in different ways. He said that reading *Awareness of Dying* (Glaser & Strauss, 1965) was like walking slowly around a statue, studying it from a variety of interrelated views. (Keeping the "secret" of anticipated death from a dying person was the phenomenon-statue.) On the other hand, reading *Time for Dying* (Glaser & Strauss, 1968), which discussed the successive steps in hospitalized dying, was like walking downhill step by step. The ordering of chapters in each monograph was what principally conveyed the feeling of their respective architectures. The structure of a recent book written by us (Corbin & Strauss, 1988) was envisioned in terms of another metaphor before we even began to outline the manuscript. Imagine walking into a house, we said: First a visitor would enter and pass through a porch, then the foyer, then enter a large room that had two prominent subsections, then leave the house through the back door. Then he or she would walk slowly around the entire house, looking into the main room through several different windows but now observing carefully the relationships of the various objects in the room. When our manuscript was finished, its form corresponded to this spatial metaphor: An introduction, a preliminary chapter, a large theoretical section composed of three chapters, then another long section consisting of several chapters that elaborated and drew implications from the theoretical formulations presented earlier.

If faced with writing a thesis, you may find this third procedure (visualization) difficult to use. After all, theses in most university departments are required to have fairly standard formats, even when presenting qualitative research. Theses tend to begin with an introductory chapter, followed by a review of the literature, then findings (in two or three chapters), and finally the summary/conclusions/implications. For all that, a thesis writer may be able to think architecturally about the middle (content) chapters. At any rate, when constructing a thesis based on the grounded theory approach, a researcher should greatly **rely on the first two procedures touched on above**: (1) developing a clear analytic story through the diagrams, sorting and, of course, continued thought; then (2) working out provisionally a main outline that will fully incorporate all important components of that story.

What to Write?

However, in writing grounded theory theses, one especially difficult problem may be encountered. Its source is the fairly complex analysis generated through the entire research process. The big question is then: What of all this analysis do you write? After all, the standard format for writing theses does not leave much actual space—short of writing a much larger thesis than you wish, or have time, to write—so how to compress most of what you now know? In short, how much depth does one go into when reporting the research? The answer is that first you must know what your main analytic message will be. Then you must give enough conceptual detail to convey this to readers. The actual form of your central chapters should be consonant with the analytic message and its components.

This answer nevertheless fails to specify, whether for writing a thesis or monograph, how to select any particular "conceptual detail" from among all the other details. While nobody who is unfamiliar with your study can specify this beforehand, first of all you must at least present the analytic story.

This will of course include the core category. Next, you might follow Barney Glaser's counsel that the:

> general, grounded, most relevant properties of the core [category] are discussed [first], to give the fullest meaning of its . . . nature. Then from these properties . . . select those that will be developed in the [introductory theoretical] chapter in relation to the problem. Thus, typically one discusses in a chapter or page [of a thesis or monograph] only one of many properties of a core category. (Glaser, 1978, p. 131)

Special Issues for Thesis Writers

Writing a grounded theory thesis "right" is, on the face of it, even more complicated than writing up the more usual types of qualitative research. Nevertheless, the various procedures discussed in earlier chapters, plus those discussed just above, should make your task considerably easier.

Here are a couple of additional points concerning the writing of theses and monographs in the grounded theory mode. Since you have never written one, **you have to learn two skills simultaneously.** One is how to present in written form the various analyses generated by this complex research process, and to integrate them all—again in written form. Of course, you have done much of this in your cumulative memos. Although sections of these memos can be incorporated virtually intact in the manuscript, nevertheless the memos were not written for communicating with readers. So, though you have learned to think in analytically complex ways, you still have to develop adequate communicative skills for conveying the sense of your analyses. Writing and thinking have now to play back and forth in your head and on the page. As you do this, while writing a chapter or two, you should become increasingly better at both of these specialized skills. Understandably, in the initial phases of writing you may have to be patient while you work hard at developing these interrelated skills. While writing the first chapters, if you find the going tough then at least you can look forward to easier weeks ahead. As further consolation, you can tell yourself with some truth that the papers and monographs to follow (and they should!) will generally be less difficult to write.

The Issue of Self-Confidence

The increasing ease in accomplishing what is, after all, quite specialized writing is also related to the issue of a researcher's confidence in his or her own analytic and compositional abilities. In this regard, we shall quote from one of our books since the quotation expresses succinctly what you as an inexperienced researcher—especially in grounded theory studies—are likely to experience. The quotation refers more to analysis than writing, but in writing itself the two skills are, as we have noted, tightly joined.

> Researchers may find themselves blocked in beginning to write, let alone during the writing itself, if they lack confidence in their analysis. Do I really have it right? Have I left out something essential? Do I really have the core category? And if yes, still, do I have all of this in enough detail (conceptual density)?

> The answers may be, yes, no, or maybe! But the issue here is not whether the analysis has been adequately and sufficiently done, but confidence that one really knows the answers to those questions. Even experienced researchers may not always be certain before they have chewed on their suspended pencils long enough to know where precisely are the holes—or to be certain that, after review, they know there are no important holes—in their analysis. Whether experienced or inexperienced, a common tactic for

reducing uncertainty is "the trial"—try it out on other people, individuals, or groups, informally or formally.

Seminars can give presenters confidence in their analyses, whether in preliminary or almost final form, as well as confidence in the analyses embodied in their writing. Speeches given at conventions, if favorably received, can add further validation of an analysis and its effective reflection in readable prose.

Nevertheless, when approaching or even during the writing period, there is almost invariably a considerable amount of anxiety about whether this can be, or is being, accomplished effectively. After all, some people are perfectionists and cannot seem to settle for less than an ideal performance. That can mean, of course, no performance at all or a greatly delayed one. Others lack some measure of confidence in themselves generally, and this spills over into questions about ability to accomplish this particular kind of task.

This anxiety and anguish . . . can be further mitigated (also) by writing a paper or two before embarking—at least, seriously—on the long and major writing task . . . getting a paper or two accepted for publication can give a considerable boost to flagging confidence or lingering doubts about one's ability at research (and writing it up effectively). (Strauss, 1987, pp. 259-260)

Letting Go

Having edited what probably should be the final draft, a researcher can also have difficulty in "letting go" with regard to the manuscript. This problem is due not so much to a lack of self-confidence, though it can be that, but to a temporary failure of nerve: "Have I really got the last details in? Got them right?" These doubts are stimulated by the almost inevitable discovery of additional detail, both conceptual and editorial, and the relocation and rephrasing that occurs during each rewriting of a draft. Part of an increasing maturity as a research-writer is to understand that no manuscript is ever finished. If fortunate enough not to have a personal, departmental or publisher's deadline, then you may profit from not looking at the "final" draft for some weeks or even months, in order to get a bit of editorial and analytic distance from it. Also, a colleague or two who might read part or even all of the manuscript usually will improve its quality. (However, beware of too harsh a judgment or some measure of misunderstanding; but if the latter, then you should wonder why the misunderstanding occurred.) Eventually you do have to let go, physically and psychologically, having convinced yourself that the manuscript is as finished as it ever will be; unless this is your thesis, and then you will surely make it into a better product if you decide to convert it into a book.

The logic of letting go is that your theoretical formulations are only part of a cumulative stream of such formulations, to which you yourself may return later to criticize; or incorporate some of these formulations in your later work, just as you would for other people's formulations or criticisms. **The psychology of this letting go** is, however, more complex. Basically it comes down to avoiding the trap of dreaming of *the* perfect manuscript, and allowing yourself instead to be open to new projects, new ideas, new data. "Oh" (you might protest here), "but I might do sloppy work if I don't linger over it." Linger, yes, but strike a balance between profitable reworking of drafts and cutting loose from them. How to do this cannot be conveyed in the abstract. Of course, an experienced researcher who actually knows your work might help with this problem, but in the end you must rely on your own inner sense of psychological rightness.

If you are writing a dissertation and are fortunate enough to study in a department that allows a less stilted thesis format, then you can write for wider audiences than your committee or the wider departmental faculty. Moreover, book publishers usually reject out of hand most theses sent to them as possible publications. So, if you are allowed to write a thesis in a style that approximates a monograph, then the conversion to a potential publication is rendered that much easier.

Audiences

There is also the question of a writer's conception of the audiences for his or her thesis. Perhaps this issue is less complicated than for other forms of publication (this will be discussed below) and for speeches, but it is one that plagues many students. After all, the immediate readers are the thesis advisor and other members of the doctoral committee. If they do not approve of the dissertation then the entire enterprise will be a personal disaster. When doctoral committees consist of faculty who strongly disagree on their criteria for adequate work, then students know they can be hurt by these methodological discrepancies. If fortunate or astute, students choose committee members who agree among themselves or are sufficiently impressed by the draft presented to them, or perhaps are so disinterested or so unversed in the substantive area that they accept the dissertation. There is no tried and true rule to suggest how this variable situation can be managed. Our best counsel is to choose if possible a supportive yet critical advisor, and to write as good a manuscript as possible. If you produce solid research then you are likely to earn your degree, unless none of the committee members can countenance qualitative research. If that is a possibility, then you should strive to keep the number of such potentially adverse critics on your committee to a minimum.

There are some crucial differences between monographs and theses, though in the pages above we have referred to them separately and together. Chief among their differences is that the discussion in a monograph should be conceptually fuller— done in greater depth and detail. Since there is more space and the constraints of the thesis format are absent, an author is freer to develop an analytic message. Moreover, the monograph can be more complex, not only in more extensive elaboration of categories and their relationships but in presenting a much greater amount of substantive material. The latter may include case studies and even long quotations from interviews, field notes, and documents. The author may always choose to digress sometimes, discussing minor and side issues, as long as these are consonant with the main thrust of the monograph. Also, some issues are likely to be explored that were omitted from the more restricted dissertation or not fully worked out during the dissertation research. Inconsistencies that crept into the more hurried writing of the thesis should be corrected in the monograph. Dissertation committees tend to look favorably on "findings," whereas the readers of monographs are more likely to appreciate or at least accept an analytically based argument, as well as a broader discussion of the research materials.

The author of a monograph has also more latitude in choosing a style of presentation. In some part the style should depend on the author's message, and in some part on a conception of the audiences for the message. Are the readers restricted to disciplinary or professional colleagues, or to some types of them; or does one hope to have readers from several fields, including perhaps their practitioners? How about if one has a lay readership in mind? For a monograph to be maximally effective, its author should ask: "What do I wish to say to each of these audiences—or if several, then how do I manage to reach each; how do I combine styles into a single integrated one?" In short, the style and shape of presentation should be sensitive to and reflect the targeted audiences.

Suppose you are addressing both your disciplinary colleagues and readers who are native to the substantive area that you have been studying? To reach both audiences will call for considerable thought about and skill in the use of vocabulary, terminology, case materials, overall mood, and other aspects of writing style. Many monographs published by sociologists have both collegial and native readers as expected audiences. (Among the grounded theory studies, see Biernacki, 1986; Fagerhaugh & Strauss, 1977; Fagerhaugh, Strauss, Suczek, & Wiener, 1987; Glaser, 1976; Glaser & Strauss, 1965, 1968; Strauss, Fagerhaugh, Suczek, & Wiener, 1985.) Sometimes the expected native readers will be lay people: for instance, patients and their families in a book on epileptics (Schneider & Conrad, 1983). Occasionally monographs are also written as much for lay people as for colleagues or professionals. Then they are published as trade books, as in a book on remarriage after divorce (Cauhape, 1983).

To write for multiple audiences is generally a more complicated task than only to write for one's colleagues or for those in neighboring fields. Yet many researchers are eager—or obligated by conscience—to write for more than scientific or professional readers. Sometimes too they use their research as a platform for writing books that are not monographs. One possibility is to address policy issues: This means presenting an argument, though informed by one's research and perhaps also by experiential knowledge gathered in, around, as well as through the research itself. See for instance, the authors' book on health policy (Strauss & Corbin, 1988). Or books can be written for practitioners, full of information based on research. (For a grounded theory example, see Strauss et al., 1984, on chronic illness management.) None of this precludes, of course, publishing a straightforward monograph written primarily for readers in one's own discipline or profession: Most qualitative research monographs have been written for those restricted audiences.

Converting Theses to Monographs

How is a thesis converted into a monograph? Guidelines bearing on how to do this were suggested implicitly in the preceding pages. However, the prior question that faces the author of a dissertation is whether it should be written up next in monograph form. **Several questions pertaining to this decision should be carefully thought through,** and preferably in the following order.

(1) Are the substantive materials, findings, or theoretical formulations presented in the thesis sufficiently interesting to be worth my time and effort to write up for a wider audience or audiences? Some theses are natural candidates for such presentation. (As examples, see Whyte's monograph on a street corner gang, 1955; Davis's book on recovery from polio, 1963;

Shibutani's study of a rumor, 1966; Broadhead's book on medical students, 1983; Cauhaupe's book on remarriage after a divorce, 1983; Rosenbaum's book on women drug addicts, 1981; Wiener's volume on alcoholic arenas, 1981; Star's monograph on the mind-body and brain localization controversy, 1989.) Other dissertations, no matter how important they may be to some colleagues, are not good candidates but portions of their materials are likely to be published as articles and later may be widely cited.

(2) If important, then which are the most relevant topics and conceptualizations to publish in a monograph?

(3) Do I have sufficient time and energy to translate this thesis into a monograph? Am I really still interested in this subject matter? Am I saturated, bored, with it? "Have I had it?" Is it really my forté or should I move on to other, now more interesting topics or areas? Of course sufficient interest in doing it successfully can lead to very great personal satisfaction. Part of the commitment and resulting satisfaction may also derive from a sense of obligation to audiences "out there" who ought to know about what one has discovered through the research.

(4) There is still another question that many potential authors consider: Given a certain level of interest and sufficient time and energy, is it worth writing this monograph for career purposes? In some fields, writing a monograph (or other type of research based book) is not especially important: papers published in refereed journals bring more prestige. However, colleagues in other fields, including the social sciences—especially when considering candidates when recruiting faculty or when they themselves are considered for promotion—know that monographs often weigh more heavily in the evaluation than do papers.

After considering each of these questions and perhaps others, and helped no doubt, as well as sometimes impeded or confused by the counsel of faculty advisors, friends, sponsors, or other intimates—then you are still confronted with the additional question of how to translate your thesis into a monograph. In fact, trying to answer this question is very likely to affect your decision whether to write, since you are weighing the time and effort involved if you write the monograph "in this way or that."

The actual conversion of the dissertation can be carefully guided by considerations touched on in preceding pages. You will have to think carefully about which audiences you wish to reach. This means the equally careful thinking through of what topics, or concepts, or theoretical formulations, will be of greatest interest or value to each audience. Those considerations lead to the issue of style. For instance, what format should be used? Should theoretical formulations be the major focus of the monograph and substantive materials subordinated, or should they be kept in balance? Should you argue forthrightly with existing theoretical formulations, or keep your argument low key or even implicit? Stylistic considerations of course also entail decisions about the kind and level of vocabulary to be used, modes of presenting selections from your data, the overall mood of the monograph, and so on.

Other considerations touched on earlier were that conceptual elaboration must be added to the original presentation in the thesis. You can do this by including theoretical materials already developed in your memos but omitted from the dissertation, and by thinking through aspects of your formulations that were left unclear, ambiguous, incomplete, and even inconsistent. Also, in a monograph, you probably will wish to discuss at greater length certain implications of your work with reference to the theoretical literature, as well as implications for future research, and perhaps for practitioners or policy decision makers.

Any and all of these possibilities or imperatives require—do they not?—time and effort but also considerable rethinking of your previous analyses, and the written expressions of these. Many researchers have found the experience of rewriting for a monograph tremendously rewarding. Others have translated theses into monographs primarily for career advancement and personal reputation, cashing in (literally) on that investment.

Team Publications

When a project involves two or more researchers then there is always a question of how publications are to be written by them. The answers depend, understandably, on the relationships between team members, their perceived respective abilities and interests, their responsibilities, the amount of time available to each, and so on. Some publications are written by the principal investigator of the project, with varying amounts of input by other team members. Other publications involve more truly collaborative writing, rather than just shared research. Presumably the combinations of cooperation (or noncooperation) are numerous. The same is true of papers based on the team's research.

Writing Papers for Publication

This fourth class of research based publications is scarcely a homogeneous one. The great variety of options for types of papers can be suggested graphically by a three fold breakdown of those possibilities.

(1) *For colleagues,* papers with major focus that is, alternatively:
   —theoretical
   —substantive
   —argumentive
   —methodological
(2) *For practitioners:*
   —theoretical framework for understanding clients better
   —substantive
   —practical suggestions for better procedures
   —reform of existing practices
   —broad policy suggestions

(3) *For lay readers*:
 —substantive
 —reform of current practices or policies
 —guidelines for how to manage better or get better service from practitioners or institutions
 —assuring readers that others share their own experience (as in living through a divorce or adopting a child)

This variety of options for papers points to differences in purposes, emphases, styles, and of course different publication outlets.

Nevertheless, your research provides a firm basis for writing all of these types of papers. You would write very different ones, and write them differently, if you did not have this hard-earned research "in you." Grounded theory research provides theoretical analyses, substantive content, and self-confidence as well. While the research itself does not tell you directly what papers to write, with what purpose, for whom, or how; none-theless the research should have given you considerable sensi-tivity to issues, audiences, and the strengths and weaknesses of actors and organizations. You will draw on this knowledge too when making decisions as to what to write, for whom, and how.

Decisions concerning those issues rest on reasoning and procedures not appreciably different than those discussed throughout this chapter. **The few important differences** can be stated briefly and are easily understood. Here are some condi-tions that may directly affect how and for whom and whether certain papers will be written:

(1) As noted earlier, researchers may decide to publish papers even relatively early during the research process. They may do this for different reasons: For instance, to present preliminary findings, or to satisfy or impress sponsors, or because they have interesting materials bearing on side issues that can easily be written up now but might not get written at a later more hectic time.

(2) Sometimes researchers write papers because they feel either obligated to publish on a given topic or because they are pressured to do so. Of course this motivation will also affect what and how a researcher writes.

(3) Researchers may also be invited to contribute papers to special issues of journals or edited volumes, because they are known to be researching in given areas. They may also be urged or be tempted to convert verbal presentations into papers, because listeners have responded well to them.

(4) Another condition that can affect the writing of a paper is the existence of a deadline for getting the finished product to an editor. For some researchers this can act as a stimulus, while others of course are daunted by any deadline.

(5) The number of pages allowed by the editor also affects whether a paper will be written—at least for this particular publication—and what will be written and how.

(6) Unless invited by an editor, there is the important decision to be made about which particular journal should be selected as a potential outlet for a given paper. Journals and papers have to be matched, otherwise time is wasted in its rejection, or worse yet the paper is accepted but for an inappropriate or insufficiently appreciative audience. Selecting an appropriate journal may be an easy task if the researcher knows that journal well, but otherwise issues of the journal should be carefully scrutinized. It helps to get the counsel, also, of people who are knowledgeable about specific journals. This is especially true when addressing audiences outside one's own field, as when a social scientist writes for a social work or medical journal.

Having noted these conditions, which are sometimes constraining but at other times stimulating, we can now discuss what else may be different about writing papers.

The most important considerations are the interrelated ones of **purpose** and **audience**. Given the variety of purposes and audiences listed above, you can see that this is the central issue facing any researcher who writes a paper. (This is true even when invited to write one.) "What" to say to "them?" Topics for some papers seem to emerge rather naturally during the research process. For instance, in our study of the chronically ill and their spouses, we were struck by the differences between highly collaborative and very conflicted couples in managing these illnesses. So, we wrote a paper on this topic relatively early in the research (Corbin & Strauss, 1984). Other such papers may be conceived of early or mid-project but do not get written until later—or even put off so long they get incorporated into the monograph. Some ideas for papers take much longer in their formulation. Perhaps this is because it requires deeper understanding of some phenomena to write about them, or more theoretical sophistication to feel comfortable in writing about them. Writing papers that suggest reforms might be delayed because researchers are unable to commit themselves to a reform role until they become sufficiently disturbed at what they are observing; or perhaps because the directions in which reform alternatives can be specified are not yet clear to them.

After one's theoretical formulations are worked out clearly, there is the temptation to present the entire framework in one long paper. For grounded theorists, this is a very difficult task to do, since the framework will be very complex, very dense with conceptualization. Our advice is not to attempt this task (as counseled earlier with regard to speeches). If you choose to, then give a frankly stripped-down version, referring readers to your forthcoming monograph. It is far better to choose one or two major categories, discussing their properties and perhaps interrelationships with two or three others at most. In additional papers, you can highlight a different category or two categories.

For instance, one of the authors and his colleagues wrote a paper on the work of hospitalized patients and related their work on a couple of other types of work, like "safety work" and "comfort work" (Strauss et al., 1985). In another paper, this research team wrote about the work of staff on intensive care units, focusing primarily on their safety work, especially in relation to their continuous work with medical equipment that was so potentially hazardous, as well as potentially sustaining of the infants (Wiener, Fagerhaugh, Strauss, & Suczek, 1979).

Other papers can be written around methodological issues or around policy issues. Then the theoretical materials will be kept subordinate but still give coloration to the main line of your discussion. For instance, a methodological focus may need both substantive and theoretical illustration to make sense to the reader. Policy arguments not only can be buttressed by data but can be explicitly or implicitly underpinned by a theoretical framework.

For instance, the authors gave an argument and suggestions for reform of the American health care system (Strauss & Corbin, 1988). These were based on criticism of the dominant acute care orientation of health professionals and institutions despite the prevalence of chronic illness today, a type of illness that has multiple phases each of which requires a different type of care.

To return to our suggestion that a theoretically oriented article be restricted in the number of categories or ideas discussed, the question as usual is how is that discussion to be developed? The same general answer can be given as when writing chapters of a monograph, but modified for purposes of writing a paper. First, you decide on what you wish to focus. What is your theoretical story? This decision may arise during the course of the research, or it may actually be prompted by thinking about your last integrative diagram or prior sorting of memos. You work out the details of conceptual relationships through the same processes of sorting and thinking about your materials (theoretical and substantive). Either before that actual working out of details or after having done much of this, you construct an outline of a paper. Just as with an outline for a monograph, you may wish to get some distance from this outline by waiting some days or weeks before returning to scrutinize it. As you write the subsections, **reviewing** and **sorting** will help to jog your memory and fill in additional detail.

One danger, however, that you must avoid is permitting too much detail to flood your thinking. If so, your attempts to crowd too much into the short space of a paper may either discourage you or at least impede the clarity of your exposition. The working guideline here for what goes into your paper and what is left out—even reluctantly or ruthlessly suppressed—is in the form of a dual question: Do I need this detail in order to maximize the clarity of the analytic discussion, and/or to achieve maximum substantive understanding? The first part of the question pertains to the analysis itself. The second pertains mainly to inclusion of data in the form of quotations and case materials.

As with monographs and theses, the drafts can be given a trial with friends and colleagues, and even with accommodating practitioners or lay people if the materials pertain to them. Again, you may wish to have drafts scrutinized by a writing group or a student research group if you belong to one. You also need to incorporate relevant literature. If it is a theoretical paper, you may wish to think through its implications for recommendations about changed policies or practices in the area that you have been studying.

Then, when "finally" finished, and even more finally published, you should already be on your way to thinking about, outlining, and beginning to write the next publication!

Summary

Doing presentations and publishing the findings of research presents a challenge to the researcher. With so much complex material available, how does one make choices about what to present, to whom, and how? Generally, in a verbal presentation or article, it is preferable to present in depth only one main concept (category) with maybe one or two others woven in as or related features. In monographs, one has a wider range of possibilities, but even here the writer should carefully think through the logical order of the material before doing a detailed outline. Theses present problems of their own for a standard format must be followed. Again, the writer must carefully think through how much detail to present and how to break up the material so as to best present the conceptual scheme while still retaining flow and continuity. This chapter suggests procedures to aid in these presentations.

14

Criteria for Judging a
Grounded Theory Study

A qualitative study can be evaluated accurately only if its procedures are sufficiently **explicit** so that readers of the resulting publication can assess their appropriateness. Also, the scientific canons (research standards) that the researcher has assumed should be **appropriate** to the study. What, then, do you need to know in order to judge these matters?

Scientific Canons and Qualitative Research

Some qualitative researchers maintain that the canons or standards by which quantitative studies are judged are quite inappropriate to qualitative studies (see Agar, 1986; Guba, 1981; Kirk & Miller, 1986). Probably most qualitative researchers believe these particular canons must at least be modified to fit qualitative research. Grounded theorists share their conviction that the usual canons of "good science" should be retained, but **require redefinition in order to fit the realities of qualitative research, and the complexities of social phenomena** that we seek to understand. The usual scientific canons include: significance, theory-observation compatibility, generalizability, consistency, reproducibility, precision, and verification. (There is a succinct overview of these canons in Gortner & Schultz, 1988, p. 204.) These canons are so much taken for granted by physical and biological scientists, that even philosophers of science do not explicitly discuss most of them except for verification. However, other canons—like precision, consistency, and relevance—are implicitly assumed (Popper, 1959).

The dangers that must be guarded against by qualitative researchers when using such terms lie in their more positivistic connotations, and those derived from a too literal reading of physical and biological science literature. Nor is there any reason to define or use those terms in accordance with the definitions and usage of quantitative social researchers. Every mode of discovery develops its own standards—and **procedures** for achieving them. (For a good discussion, see Diesing, 1971.) What is important is that all of these criteria are made explicit.

For instance, take the canon of reproducibility. Ordinarily this means that any given study—a physical experiment for instance—is capable of being replicated, so if the findings of the original study are reproduced in the succeeding one(s), then they are additionally credible. However, probably no theory that deals with a social/psychological phenomenon is actually reproducible, insofar as finding new situations or other situations whose conditions exactly match those of the original study, though many major conditions may be similar. Unlike study of a physical phenomenon, it is very difficult to set up experimental or other designs in which one can re-create all of the original conditions and control all of the extraneous variables that may impinge upon the social/psychological phenomenon under investigation.

Another way of denoting reproducibility is as follows. Given the same theoretical perspective of the original researcher and following the same general rules for data gathering and analysis, plus a similar set of conditions, another investigator should be able to come up with the same theoretical explanation about the given phenomenon. Whatever discrepancies that arise can be worked out through reexamination of the data and identification of the different conditions that may be operating in each case.

To continue with illustrations of how the usual canons are redefined for qualitative research, consider next the canon of generalizability. The purpose of a grounded theory is to specify the conditions that give rise to specific sets of action/interaction pertaining to a phenomenon and the resulting consequences. It is generalizable to those specific situations only. Naturally, the more systematic and widespread the theoretical sampling, the more conditions and variations that will be discovered and built into the theory, therefore the greater its generalizability (also precision, and predictive capacity). If the original theory fails to account for variation uncovered through additional research, these new specificities can be added as amendments to the original formulation.

We have only illustrated the necessity for redefining the usual canons with the two just touched on (reproducibility and generalizability), since elsewhere we have discussed in detail other important ones, in connection with grounded theory (Corbin & Strauss, 1990).

Criteria for Evaluating a Grounded Theory

We will, however, discuss some important evaluative criteria for judging research. What research? The answer is: Both your own and that of other researchers, when they claim to use grounded theory methods. These criteria should also guide the formulation of proposals written for funding agencies. Like other researchers, grounded theory researchers must address questions about sampling, analytic procedures, validity, and so on. (Presumably the representatives of funding agencies can also utilize the methodological guidelines given in this chapter for judging proposals purporting to use grounded theory methods.) The success of a research project is, after all, judged by its products. Except in unusual instances when these are only orally presented, the findings, theoretical formulations, and conclusions, as well as study design and procedures, are judged through publication. Yet, how are these to be evaluated and by what criteria?

In judging a research publication whose author(s) claims to generate, elaborate, or "test" a theory, you should distinguish clearly among these issues. First, judgments are made about the validity, reliability, and credibility of the **data** (Guba, 1981; Kidder, 1981; Kirk & Miller, 1986; Le Compte & Goetz, 1982; Miles & Huberman, 1984; Sandelowski, 1986). Second, judgments are made about the adequacy of the **research process** through which the theory is generated, elaborated, or tested. Third, judgments are made about the **empirical grounding** of the research findings.

Criteria for judging the data have been much discussed in the literature (see besides the above citations, any fieldwork text). It is the adequacy of a study's research process and the grounding of its findings that we will be concerned with here.

The Research Process

In a grounded theory publication, the reader should be able to make judgments about some of the components of the research process that led to the publication. However, even in a monograph—which after all consists primarily of theoretical formulations and analyzed data—there may be no way that readers can accurately judge how the researcher carried out the analysis. They are not actually present during the actual analytic sessions, and the monograph does not necessarily help them imagine these sessions or their sequence. To remedy this, it would be useful for readers to be given certain kinds of information bearing on the criteria given below. The detail need not be great even in a monograph, but enough to give some reasonably good grounds for judging the adequacy of the research process as such. The kinds of needed information are presented below in question form, their answers indicating how they might serve as evaluative criteria.

> Criterion #1: How was the original sample selected? What grounds?
>
> Criterion #2: What major categories emerged?
>
> Criterion #3: What were some of the events, incidents, actions, and so on (as indicators) that pointed to some of these major categories?
>
> Criterion #4: On the basis of what categories did theoretical sampling proceed? That is, how did theoretical formulations guide some of the data collection? After the theoretical sampling was done, how representative did these categories prove to be?
>
> Criterion #5: What were some of the hypotheses pertaining to conceptual relations (that is, among categories), and on what grounds were they formulated and tested?
>
> Criterion #6: Were there instances when hypotheses did not hold up against what was actually seen? How were these discrepancies accounted for? How did they affect the hypotheses?
>
> Criterion #7: How and why was the core category selected? Was this collection sudden or gradual, difficult or easy? On what grounds were the final analytic decisions made?

We realize certain of these criteria would be regarded as unconventional (for instance, theoretical rather than types of statistical sampling, or the injunction to be explicit about accounting for discrepancies) by most quantitative and even many qualitative researchers. Yet these are essential to evaluating grounded theory studies. If a grounded theory researcher provides this information, readers can use these criteria to assess the adequacy of the researcher's complex coding procedure. Detail given in this way would be supplemented with cues that could, at least in longer publications, be read as

pointing to extremely careful and thorough tracking of indicators, of conscientious and imaginative theoretical sampling,
and so on.

Next we give a series of questions that are also equivalent to
a set of criteria concerning empirical grounding of the study.

Empirical Grounding of the Study

Criterion #1: Are Concepts Generated?

Since the basic building blocks of any grounded theory (indeed any scientific theory) is a set of concepts grounded in the
data, the first questions to be asked of any publication are: Does
it generate (via coding) or at least use concepts, and what is
or are their source or sources? If concepts are drawn from
common usage (such as, "uncertainty") but not put to technical
use, then these are not concepts in the sense of being part of a
grounded theory, for they are not actually grounded in the
data themselves. In any monograph that purports to present
theoretical interpretations of data based on grounded theory
analysis, one can make a quick, if very crude, assessment of
its concepts merely by checking the index for concepts, determining whether these seem to be technical or common sense
ones, and whether there are many of them. For a fuller assessment of those points, one must at least scan the book.

Criterion #2: Are the Concepts Systematically Related?

The name of the scientific game is systematic conceptualization through conceptual linkages. So, the questions to ask here
of a grounded theory publication are whether such linkages
have been made and do they seem to be grounded in the data?
Furthermore, are the linkages systematically carried out? As
in other qualitative writing, the linkages are unlikely to be
presented as a listing of hypotheses or in proportional or other

formal terms, but will be woven throughout the text of the publication.

Criterion #3: Are There Many Conceptual Linkages and Are the Categories Well Developed? Do They Have Conceptual Density?

A grounded theory should be tightly linked, both in terms of categories to their subcategories and between the several categories in the final integration. This is done of course in terms of the paradigm features—conditions, context, action/interaction (including strategies), and consequences. Also categories should be theoretically dense (have many properties that are dimensionalized). It is the tight linkages, in terms of the paradigm features and density of the categories, that give a theory its **explanatory power**. Without these, the theory is less than satisfactory.

Criterion #4: Is Much Variation Built Into the Theory?

Some qualitative studies report only about a single phenomenon and establish only a few conditions under which it appears; also they specify only a few actions/interactions that characterize it, and a limited number or range of consequences. By contrast, a grounded theory monograph should be judged in terms of the range of its variations, and the **specificity** with which these are spelled out in relation to the data that are their source. In a published paper, the range of variations touched upon may be more limited, but the author should at least suggest that the fuller study include their specification.

Criterion #5: Are the Broader Conditions That Affect the Phenomenon Under Study Built Into Its Explanation?

The grounded theory mode of research requires that the explanatory conditions be brought into analysis and not be restricted only to those that seem to have immediate bearing on the phenomenon under study. That is, the analysis should not be so "microscopic" as to disregard conditions that derive from more "macroscopic" sources: for instance, those such as economic conditions, social movements, trends, cultural values, and so forth.

Also, these must not simply be listed as background material but **directly linked to phenomenon** through their effect on action/interaction, and through these latter to consequences. Therefore, any grounded theory publication that either omits these broader conditions or fails to explicate their specific connections to the phenomenon under investigation, falls short in its empirical grounding. In other words, **whether or not the author explicitly mentions the conditional matrix** (see Chapter 10), **in effect it should be operative in the analysis**.

Criterion #6: Has Process Been Taken Into Account?

Identifying and specifying change or movement in the form of process is an important part of grounded theory research. Any change must be linked to the conditions that gave rise to it. Recollect from Chapter 9 that process may be described as stages or phases, and also as fluidity or movement of action/interaction over the passage of time in response to prevailing conditions.

Criterion #7: Do the Theoretical Findings Seem Significant and to What Extent?

It is entirely possible to complete a grounded theory study, or any study, yet not produce findings that are significant. If the researcher simply follows the grounded theory procedures/canons without imagination or insight into what the data are reflecting—because he or she fails to see what they are really saying except in terms of trivial or well-known phenomena—then the published findings can be judged as failing on this criterion.

Remember that there is an interplay between the researcher and the data, and no method, certainly not the grounded theory one, can ensure that the interplay will be creative. This depends on three characteristics of the researcher: analytic ability, theoretical sensitivity, and sensitivity to the subtleties of the action/interaction (plus sufficient writing ability to convey the findings). Of course, a creative interplay also depends on the other pole of the researcher-data equation: The quality of data collected or utilized. An unimaginative analysis may in a technical sense be adequately grounded in the data, but actually it is insufficiently grounded for the researcher's theoretical purposes. This is because the researcher either does not draw on the fuller resources of data or fails to push data collection far enough.

This double set of criteria, for the research process and for the empirical grounding of the theoretical findings, bears directly on the issues of how verified any given grounded theory study is and how this is to be ascertained. When the study is published, if components of the research process are clearly laid out and if there are sufficient cues in the publication itself, then the presented theory or theoretical formulations can be assessed in terms of degrees of plausibility. We can judge under what conditions the theory might fit with "reality," give understanding, and be useful (practically and in theoretical terms).

A Final Note

You should keep in mind two additional comments about evaluative criteria. First, these criteria should not be read as hard and fast evaluative rules, either for you as a researcher or for you as a reader who is judging other's research publications. The criteria are meant as **guidelines**. New areas of investigation may require that the procedures and evaluative criteria be modified to fit the circumstances of the research. Imaginative researchers, who are wrestling with unusual or creative use of materials will, at times, depart somewhat from what can be termed "authoritative" guidelines for procedures. **Having said this, we strongly urge you to adhere to these major criteria unless there are very good reasons for not doing so.** In such unusual cases, you should know precisely how and why you did depart from the criteria, say so in your writing, and leave it up to readers to judge the credibility of your theory.

Second, we suggest that you **indicate what your procedural operations were, even if briefly**, especially in longer publications. These would include a listing of any special procedures or procedural steps taken in addition to those discussed in this book. This would help readers to judge the overall adequacy of your research. It would also make readers more aware of how this particular research differs from that done when using other modes of qualitative research. In doing this, you are rendered more aware of precisely what your operations have been, and their possible inadequacies. In other words, you are able to identify and convey what were the inevitable limitations of your study.

Summary

Every research study, qualitative or quantitative, must be evaluated in terms of the specific canons and procedures of the research method that was used to generate the findings. Evaluative criteria specific to grounded theory have been developed by the authors. These criteria should be useful not only for those desirous of judging their own or their colleagues' work, but also by those who sit on editorial boards and funding agencies, who also must evaluate grounded theory studies.

It is no linguistic accident that "building," "construction," "work," designate both a process and its finished product. Without the meaning of the verb that of the noun remains blank.

John Dewey, *Art as Experience*, 1934, p. 51

References

Agar, M. (1986). *Speaking of ethnography*. Beverly Hills, CA: Sage.

Becker, H. (1970). *Sociological work: Method and substance*. New Brunswick, NJ: Transaction.

Becker, H. (1982). *Art worlds*. Berkeley, CA: University of California Press.

Becker, H. (1986a). *Doing things together: Selected papers*. Evanston, IL: Northwestern University Press.

Becker, H. (1986b). *Writing for social scientists*. Chicago: University of Chicago Press.

Biernacki, P. (1986). *Pathways from heroin addiction*. Philadelphia, PA: Temple University Press.

Blumer, H. (1931). Science without concepts. *American Journal of Sociology, 36*, 515-533.

Blumer, H. (1969). *Symbolic interaction*. Englewood Cliffs, NJ: Prentice-Hall.

Broadhead, R. (1983). *Private lives and professional identity of medical students*. New Brunswick, NJ: Transaction Books.

Cauhape, E. (1983). *Fresh starts: Men and women after divorce*. New York: Basic Books.

Charmaz, K. (1983). The grounded theory method: An explication and interpretation. In R. Emerson (Ed.), *Contemporary field research* (pp. 109-126). Boston: Little, Brown.

Corbin, J. (1987). Women's perceptions and management of a pregnancy complicated by chronic illness. *Health Care for Women International, 84*, 317-37.

Corbin, J., & Strauss, A. (1984). Collaboration: Couples working together to manage chronic illness. *Image, 16*, 109-115.

Corbin, J., & Strauss, A. (1988). *Unending work and care: Managing chronic illness at home.* San Francisco, CA: Jossey-Bass.

Corbin, J., & Strauss, A. (1990). Grounded theory method: Procedures, canons, and evaluative criteria. *Qualitative Sociology.* Forthcoming.

Corbin, J., & Strauss, A. (1991). Comeback: Overcoming disability. In G. Albrecht & J. Levy (Eds.), *Advances in medical sociology* (Vol. 2) Greenwich, CT: JAI Press.

Davis, F. (1963). *Passage through crisis.* Indianapolis, IN: Bobbs-Merrill.

Denzin, N. (1970). *The research act.* Chicago: Aldine.

Dewey, J. (1934). *Art as experience.* New York: Minton, Balch.

Diesing, P. (1971). *Patterns of discovery in the social sciences.* Chicago: Aldine.

Drake, S. (1957). *Discoveries and opinions of Galileo.* Garden City, NY: Doubleday Anchor Books.

Fagerhaugh, S., & Strauss, A. (1977). *The politics of pain management: Staff-patient interaction.* Menlo Park, CA: Addison-Wesley.

Fagerhaugh, S., Strauss, A., Suzcek, B., & Wiener, C. (1987). *Hazards in hospital care.* San Francisco: Jossey-Bass.

Fielding, N., & Fielding, J. (1986). *Linking data.* Beverly Hills, CA: Sage.

Fujimura, J. (1987). Constructing doable problems in cancer research: Articulating alignment. *Social Studies of Science, 17*, 257-93.

Glaser, B. (1963). The use of secondary analysis by the independent researcher. *American Behavioral Scientist, 11-14.*

Glaser, B. (1972). *Experts and laymen: The Patsy and the subcontractor.* Mill Valley, CA: Sociology Press.

Glaser, B. (1978). *Theoretical sensitivity.* Mill Valley, CA: Sociology Press.

Glaser, B., & Strauss, A. (1965). *Awareness of dying.* Chicago: Aldine.

Glaser, B., & Strauss, A. (1967). *The discovery of grounded theory.* Chicago: Aldine.

Glaser, B., & Strauss, A. (1968). *Time for dying.* Chicago: Aldine.

Gortner, S., & Schultz, P. (1988). Approaches to nursing science methods. *Image, 20*, 22-23.

Guba, E. (1981). Criteria for assessing the trustworthiness of naturalistic inquiries. *ETC, 19*, 75-91.

Hammersley, M., & Atkinson, P. (1983). *Ethnography: Principles in practice.* New York: Tavistock.

Hughes, E. (1971). *The sociological eye.* Chicago: Aldine. Reprinted. New Brunswick. NJ: Transaction, 1987.

Johnson, J. (1975). *Doing field research.* New York: Free Press.

Kidder, L. (1981). Qualitative research and quasi-experimental frameworks. In M. Brewer & B. Collings (Eds.), *Scientific inquiry and the social sciences.* San Francisco, CA: Jossey-Bass.

Kirk, J., & Miller, M. (1986). *Reliability, validity and qualitative research.* Beverly Hills, CA: Sage.

Kvale, S. (1989). To validate is to question. In S. Kvale (Ed.), *Issues of validity in qualitative research* (pp. 73-92). Lund, Sweden: Studentlitteratur.

Le Compte, N., & Gietz, J. (1982). Problems of reliability and validity in ethnographic research. *Review of Educational Research, 52,* 31-60.

Lofland, J. (1971). *Analyzing social settings.* Belmont, CA: Wadsworth.

Miles, M. (1983). Mixing qualitative and quantitative methods: Triangulation in action. In J. Van Maanen (Ed.), *Qualitative methodology.* Beverly Hills, CA: Sage.

Miles, M., & Huberman, A. (1984). *Qualitative data analysis.* Beverly Hills, CA: Sage.

Pfaffenberger, B. (1988). *Microcomputer applications in qualitative research.* Newbury Park, CA: Sage.

Popper, K. (1959). *The logic of scientific discovery.* New York: Basic Books.

Rapport, S. & Wright, W. (Eds.). (1964). *Science: Methods and meaning.* New York: Washington Square Press.

Rosenbaum, M. (1981). *Women on heroin.* New Brunswick, NJ: Rutgers University Press.

Sandelowski, M. (1986). The problem of rigor in qualitative research. *Advances in Nursing Science, 8,* 27-37.

Schatzman, L., & Strauss, A. (1973). *Field research: Strategies for a natural sociology.* Englewood Cliffs, NJ: Prentice-Hall.

Schneider, J., & Conrad, P. (1983). *Having epilepsy: The experience and control of illness.* Philadelphia, PA: Temple University.

Seyle, H. (1956). *The stress of life.* New York: McGraw Hill.

Shibutani, T. (1966). *Improvised news: A sociological study of rumor.* Indianapolis, IN: Bobbs-Merrill.

Star, S. L. (1989). *Regions of the mind: Brain research and the quest for scientific certainty.* Stanford, CA: Stanford University Press.

Strauss, A. (1978). *Negotiations.* San Francisco: CA: Jossey-Bass.

Strauss, A. (1982). Interorganizational negotiation. *Urban Life, 11,* 350-67.

Strauss, A. (1985). Work and the division of labor. *Sociological Quarterly, 26,* 1-19.

Strauss, A. (1987). *Qualitative analysis for social scientists.* New York: Cambridge University Press.

Strauss, A., Bucher, R., Ehrlich, D., Schatzman, L., & Sabshin, M. (1964). *Psychiatric ideologies and institutions.* Glencoe, IL: Free Press.

Strauss, A., & Corbin, J. (1988). *Shaping a new health care system.* San Francisco, CA: Jossey-Bass.

Strauss, A., & Corbin, J. (1989, August). *Tracing lines of conditional influence: Matrix and paths.* Paper delivered at the annual meetings of the American Sociological Society, San Francisco, California.

Strauss, A., Corbin, J., Fagerhaugh, S., Glaser, B., Maines, D., Suczek, B., & Wiener, C. (1984). *Chronic illness and the quality of life* (2nd ed.). St. Louis: Mosby.

Strauss, A., Fagerhaugh, S., Suczek, B., & Wiener, C. (1985). *The organization of medical work.* Chicago: University of Chicago Press.

Tesch, R. (1989). *Qualitative research: Analysis types and software tools.* Philadelphia, PA: Taylor and Francisc.

Whyte, W. (1955). *Street corner society.* Chicago: University of Chicago Press.

Wiener, C. (1981). *The politics of alcoholism.* New Brunswick, NJ: Transaction Books.

Wiener, C., Fagerhaugh, S., Strauss, A., & Suczek, B. (1979). Trajectories, biographies and the evolving medical technology scene: Labor and delivery and the intensive care nursery. *Sociology of Health and Illness, 1,* 261-83.

Index

About the Authors

Juliet Corbin is a lecturer in the Department of Nursing, San Jose State University, San Jose, California, and also a research associate in the Department of Social and Behavioral Sciences, University of California, San Francisco. She received her B.S.N. degree (1963) from Arizona State University, her M.S.N. degree (1972) from San Jose State University, and her D.N.S. (1981) from the University of California, San Francisco. She has authored or co-authored a number of research articles, and chapters in edited collections, and is the co-author of a research monograph, *Unending Work and Care* (1988), as well as a research-based policy volume titled *Shaping A New Health Care System* (1988). She is currently researching the role of the body in action, and engaged in the fieldwork study of the flow of work in hospitals.

Anselm Strauss is professor emeritus of sociology, Department of Social and Behavioral Sciences, University of California, San Francisco. His main research activities have been in the sociology of health and illness, and in the sociology of work/

professions. The research methods used in his studies have principally been a combination of field observation and interviews, but occasionally historical materials are used as primary data. Among his (and co-authors') books on method or monographs are: *The Discovery of Grounded Theory* (1967), *Qualitative Analysis for Social Scientists* (1987), *Awareness of Dying* (1965), *The Social Organization of Medical Work* (1985), and *Unending Work and Care* (1988). He has been a visiting professor at the Universities of Cambridge, Paris, Manchester, Constance, Adelaide, and Hagen. His current research includes studies of AIDS policy making and implementation, of the flow of work in hospitals, and of the role of the body in action.